I0145361

BREAKING ANGER'S EMBRACE

and Other Insights on the Human Condition

THOMAS SCHNEIDER, PH.D.
REFLECTS ON 40 YEARS AS A CLINICAL PSYCHOLOGIST

—᎐᎐᎐—

First Edition 2012

© 2012 Thomas Schneider, Ph.D., Author
&
© SouthForce International, LLC, Publisher

4480 South Cobb Drive, Suite H-507
Smyrna, Georgia, 30080
USA

www.southforce.com

ISBN: 978-0-9851301-8-3 (Print)
ISBN: 978-0-9851301-0-7 (eBook)

ALL RIGHTS RESERVED.

Print Version

No part of the printed form of this book may be reproduced, stored in a retrieval
system or transmitted by any means, electronic, mechanical, photocopying,
recording or otherwise, without the prior written permission of the Publisher.

E-Book Version Available

Once purchased and downloaded by purchaser, no part of the e-book may be
reproduced or transmitted to another party by any means, electronic, mechanical,
photocopying, recording or otherwise, without the prior written permission of
the Publisher.

www.breakingangersembrace.com

III

ENDORSEMENTS

In today's world, which is saturated with anger, it is a welcome relief to encounter a book such as Dr. Thomas Schneider's "Breaking Anger's Embrace". Dr. Schneider not only presents clearly his thoughts and ideas on anger, but also presents many ways to mediate and utilize this emotion. Dr. Schneider's ideas about anger were garnered over 80 years of living and 40 years of experience as a therapist, mentor to other therapists, husband, father, grandfather, Sunday school teacher, scientist, and scholar. He has contributed to Jung's ideas on the collective unconscious with his own original idea that he has termed 'the ancestral unconscious.' This represents a unique historic feature of each individual's unconscious, reflecting ancestral input into his or her current state of being. This novel idea is carried even further as he describes the genie in the bottle, the genie containing all the stopped-up creativity that individuals carry from their past ancestral history. He points out that anger can act as a stopper and prevent the individual's genie from escaping and becoming accessible to that person.

Dr. Schneider has presented the most complex ideas in simplified and easily understood ways. His Pimple Parable deals with problems inherent in children, adolescents and adults who focus their attention on minor negative aspects of themselves to the exclusion of all their positive attributes. Parents, therapists, clergy, teachers, and people dealing with personal issues and problems common to us all, will find this book useful in producing new interpersonal insights. "Breaking Anger's Embrace" can be read many times, each reading producing new insights, and it will remain a source of reference in one's library.

Ray A. Craddick, Ph.D., ABPP
Professor Emeritus of Psychology
Georgia State University

ENDORSEMENTS

A marvelous opportunity to view anger and its cohorts as a challenge for development, therapy, and change. Personally written with psychological understanding, humor, and hope for learning to manage our unawareness of feelings and their sources. This little BIG book could be seen as an "ancestral" companion to the Jungian collective unconscious. Relating emotional choices to adaptational learning is, indeed, how we humans can change how we feel about ourselves. Yes! This is uncorking the "Genie" inside our shadows.

T. Albert Davis, M.D.
Psychiatrist
Georgia

Tom Schneider left a demanding and rewarding business career to earn a doctorate in psychology and embark upon a more demanding and ultimately more rewarding adventure as a psychotherapist. In BREAKING ANGER'S EMBRACE, he provides a roadmap for living that is experience-based—he lives in the real world—and infused with the insights of the discipline he has practiced for over four decades. He is witty; he is dead serious. Above all he is respectful, always acknowledging human dignity's centrality. Analyzing anger, that anaconda of emotions whose embrace constricts and then devours its victim, he suggests techniques that will break its killing embrace. His distilled wisdom on this topic and other life issues makes his book eminently worth reading. And then reading again.

Paula Lawton Bevington
Principal, Bevington Advisors, LLC
Georgia

Through a collection of interlacing essays, Dr. Schneider shares his 40 years of experience working in family psychology. He clearly demonstrates that managing anger is not enough; family members must break the embrace of anger in order to enjoy life to its fullest.

Linda M. Johnston, Ph.D.
Executive Director
Siegel Institute for Leadership, Ethics & Character
Kennesaw State University
Georgia

ENDORSEMENTS

Dr. Schneider offers practical ways to deal with the emotion of anger. He shows you how not to allow anger to consume you. Breaking Anger's Embrace forces you to examine not only why you are angry, but it forces you to examine yourself. Perhaps you may not like what you see. This forces you to cognitively search for the true, hidden, underlying factor. This is a book for anyone who is interested in understanding their own behavior. Furthermore, it helps you understand the behavior of others. As an adult, child, and adolescent psychiatrist, I recommend this book to anyone who is trying to understand themselves.

Karl E. Douyon, M.D., M.S.
Diplomate of the American Board of Psychiatry and Neurology
Qualified Medical Examiner
California

Aren't you glad you bought this book? In only a few pages you knew you were in the capable hands of a wise old man with a twinkle in his eye who has much wisdom to pass along, such as splendid advice on how to raise your children successfully while keeping the peace or, gasp, how to teach sex education to a Sunday School class, not to mention handling anger. Breaking Anger's Embrace is a good investment in your and your family's well-being.

Joen Fagan, Ph.D.
Regents' Professor of Psychology, Emerita
Georgia State University

In Memoriam

Our daughter, Virginia (Ginnie) Schneider Bailey embodied the words, "people person" every day of her life. As a registered nurse, she worked for the incomparable Shepherd Center in Atlanta helping patients who had brain injuries or multiple sclerosis. Her caring ways also extended to animals. Ginnie was an avid supporter of The Atlanta Humane Society and helped to rescue and care for many creatures that needed a gentle touch and lots of love. We miss her beyond expression.

DEDICATION

To Ray Craddick, Ph.D.
beloved teacher, mentor, colleague, friend, and inspirer,
who said to me just three little words:
"Write a book."
So I did.

Thomas Schneider

EDITORIAL TEAM

Editor-in-Chief	Joan Thomas
Senior Copy Editor	David Compton
Copy Editor	Paula Bevington
Researchers	Lyn Zeman
	David Zeman
	Kim Luttery
Cover Designer	Richelle McCullough
Illustrators	Rashad Gibson
	Tanya Ferguson
Layout Artist	Dori Nicholson
Videographer	Joan Thomas

ACKNOWLEDGEMENTS

I completed the first draft of this collection of insights in 2008. At that time, I gave copies of it to various family members, colleagues, and friends. Their critiques (both positive and negative) contributed immensely to this current work, and they all have my deepest thanks and affection.

They are, in no particular order: Bettye Schneider, Bob Schneider, Lyn Zeman, Maggie and David Zeman, Thomas Schneider III, Ray and Noreen Craddick, Stuart Higginbotham, Tom Conley, Albert Davis, Roberta Golden, Gwen Bate, Gail Bell, Vickie Harkins, Mimi Baird, Betty Whitaker, and John Forbes. I am also grateful to my dear friends Paula Bevington and Joan Thomas for their overall editorial skills and thoughtful contributions.

Appreciation must be given also to our grandson David for his invaluable research efforts. I give special thanks to our beloved daughter Lyn for her skills of typing, editing, and her thoughtful suggestions. It must be said that she also has an uncanny ability to decipher my so-called penmanship, bless her.

A NOTE TO THE READER

When I turned eighty, I decided to write down a few of the things I have thought about, felt, and come to believe while I could still remember them.

I have been a practicing clinical psychologist for more than forty years, so most of my views on anger, communication, couples, parenting, and therapy come from practical, hands-on experience.

My views on teaching and reaching teenagers come from many years of experience as a parent, grandparent, teacher and therapist.

I discovered my "ancestral unconscious" and my "genie" when I first heard my deceased grandfather's musical force come alive within me.

HOW TO UNDERSTAND THE CONTENTS OF THIS BOOK:
Each essay or chapter is written to be read independently, so you will find some repetition of key concepts. I hope you will enjoy reading my thoughts as much as I've enjoyed collecting, recollecting, and expressing them.

Thomas Schneider

CONTENTS

1
Breaking Anger's Embrace

- He, she, it makes me angry.

- Don't get mad, get even.

- I'm not angry, I'm just hurt.

- Let it all hang out.

- Venting your anger at someone sets boundaries.

- Getting anger out is a cure for depression.

- Honest exchanges of anger improve relationships.

What do all these statements have in common? As far as I'm concerned, they are all nonsense. Why? Here are a few ironies that may help clarify my points of view.

When people say

- "It's not the money; it's the principle." *It's the money.*

- "It's not the gift; it's the thought." *It's the gift.*

- "I don't want praise, just honest criticism." *He wants praise.*

- I'm not angry; I'm just hurt." *She's angry.*

If all of this arouses your curiosity, read on.

First, let us try to define precisely what anger is. The ancient Greeks included it among the four basic humors as choleric, believing it was caused by yellow bile. Webster's Dictionary defines it as "a strong feeling of displeasure and usually of antagonism." Evolutionary theory would claim anger as a survival emotion that prepares and energizes our ability to fight. Freudian theory sees anger as a defense mechanism necessary to protect us from harm, either physical or psychological.

Second, anger covers a wide range of emotions that vary in intensity.

Schneider's Anger Intensity Scale

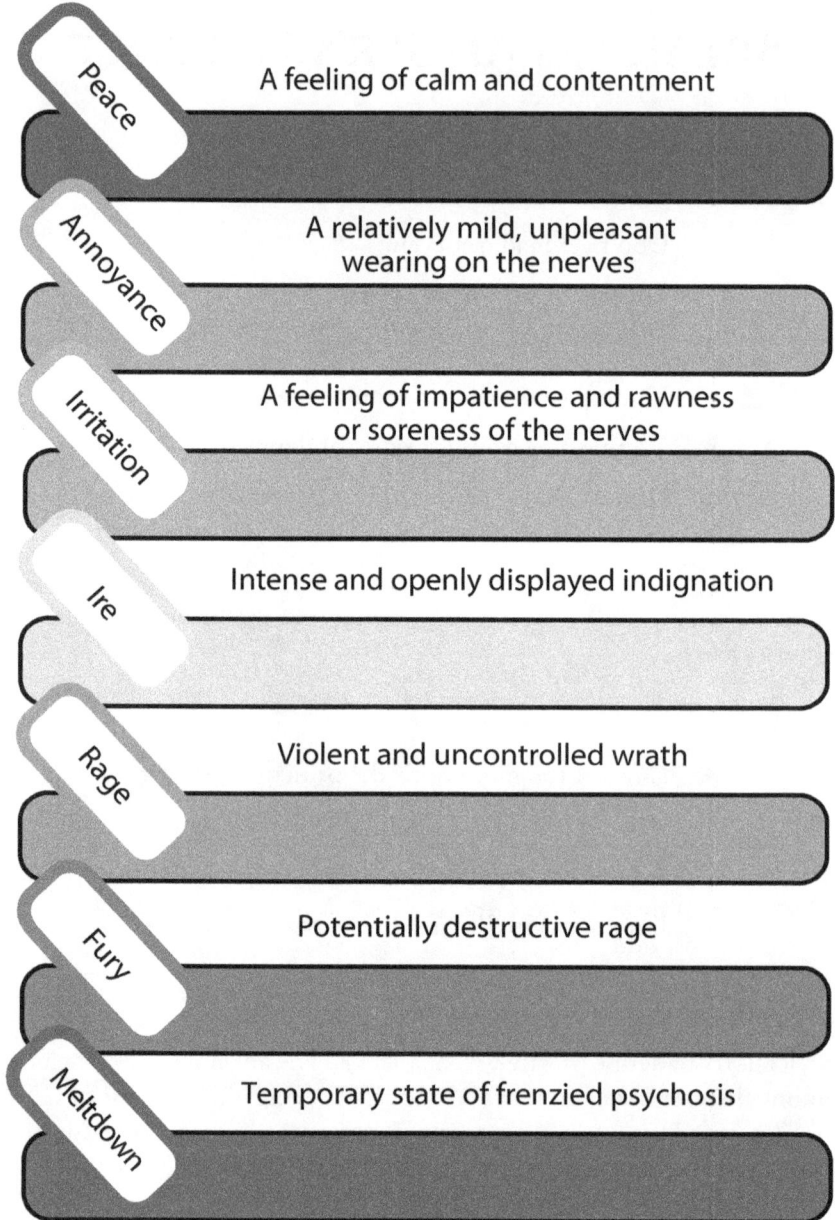

Peace — A feeling of calm and contentment

Annoyance — A relatively mild, unpleasant wearing on the nerves

Irritation — A feeling of impatience and rawness or soreness of the nerves

Ire — Intense and openly displayed indignation

Rage — Violent and uncontrolled wrath

Fury — Potentially destructive rage

Meltdown — Temporary state of frenzied psychosis

© October 2011
Thomas E. Schneider, Ph. D.

These feelings are usually accompanied by varying sensations of heat. A corresponding temperature scale might look like this:

Schneider's Anger Gauge: Temperatures

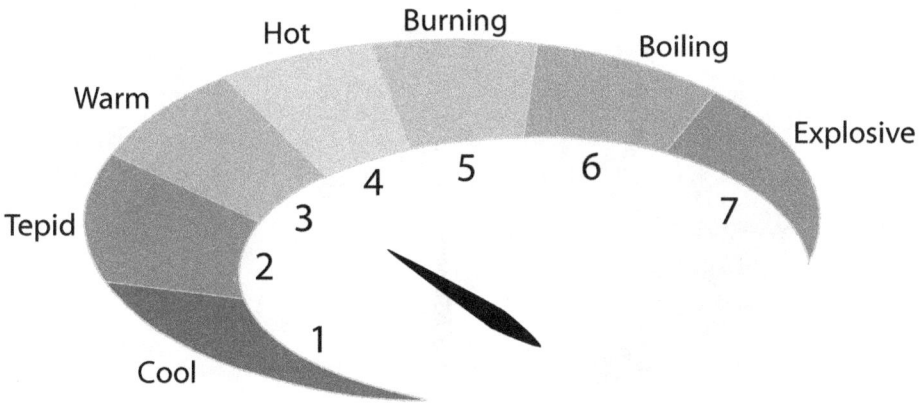

Burning

Hot

Boiling

Warm

Explosive

Tepid

5

6

4

3

7

2

1

Cool

© October 2011
Thomas E. Schneider, Ph. D.

This scale provides a qualitative and quantitative method of measuring various levels of anger and provides an indication of emotional change. Armed with these scales, angry people can monitor their states of mind and regulate their emotional temperatures.

Schneider's Anger Gauge: Emotions

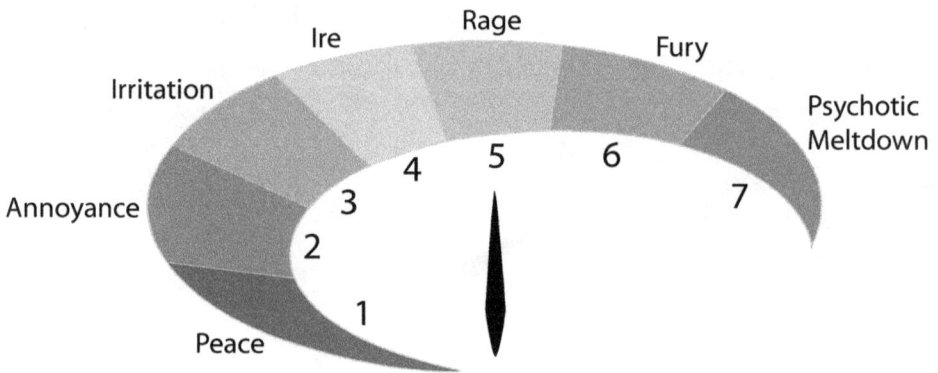

Rage

Ire

Fury

Irritation

Psychotic
Meltdown

Annoyance

4 5 6

3

7

2

1

Peace

© Ocober 2011
Thomas E. Schneider, Ph. D.

Third, anger can also be defined by type: reactive, responsive and retentive.

REACTIVE ANGER

- Reactive anger is controlled by the automatic (autonomic) nervous system. It is the usual reaction to an unpleasant circumstance such as hurt, love, fear, insult, intrusion, disappointment, embarrassment or frustration.

- Reactive anger can be intensified by factors such as fatigue, stress, depression, or pain. Also, it can be diminished by factors such as a sense of well-being; but, more about that in the next chapter.

- Reactive anger can be healthy if it is taken as a sign or warning that other feelings, of which we were not previously aware, lurk beneath it. It can also be healthy if it leads to a deeper exploration of ourselves or those who are the targets of our anger.

RESPONSIVE ANGER

Responsive anger is the angry feeling that remains after we have had time to think. Then we make a conscious choice to respond in an angry way: to get even; to stand our ground; to retaliate.

RETENTIVE ANGER

Retentive anger comes in two forms: chronic and deliberate.

CHRONIC ANGER

- Chronic anger emerges in persons who seem to have been born angry. It may be caused by a genetic personality disorder or a physiological imbalance, something awry in the person's body chemistry. It may also result from early childhood trauma—abuse, neglect, loss—a type of anger that the individual may not want to eliminate. This anger can protect against future pain, can soothe perceived injustices (righteous indignation) or can serve as an excuse for pursuing negative or destructive behaviors.

- Chronic anger is dangerous and disagreeable. It can lead to serious physical and psychological problems. It is hard to cure.

- Chronic anger can be alleviated by some medications and/ or long-term psychotherapy. Interestingly, there is not a psychiatric classification for anger itself. The closest one, which I really like, is "intermittent explosive disorder," which covers such behaviors as road rage or unexplained violent temper tantrums.

- ♦ Chronic anger is never healthy. Recent medical research has shown the high correlation between anger and heart disease and other physical or emotional problems.

DELIBERATE ANGER

- ♦ Deliberate anger is the anger we hang onto when we feel we have been hurt, disappointed, wronged, diminished, or insulted.

- ♦ Deliberate anger is probably the unhealthiest anger of all. It is in our power to change it if we choose to do so, but often we do not want to admit this fact.

- ♦ Becoming aware of the damage that deliberate anger can trigger is the first step toward doing something about it; and we may not want to do something about it. We may actually enjoy holding on to our anger, calling it resentment. Bearing a grudge lays the blame and the responsibility on someone else. This superior attitude may actually feel better to us than confronting our own underlying feelings.

- ♦ The first and most important point to remember about deliberate anger is this: *The better we feel about ourselves, the less need we have to choose to be angry and, therefore, to choose to hang onto that anger.*

Let's get one thing straight. This is not an essay on anger management. This essay addresses breaking anger's embrace, eliminating anger—*dissolving* anger. Now, why would anyone wish to juxtapose two such disparate words as "embrace" and "anger"? If we must hang onto our anger or let our anger hang onto us, wouldn't a term such as "bondage" be more appropriate? The answer is no, because it just so happens that our anger can be a very comfortable shield against other more painful emotions from which it guards us. Those emotions are fear, shame, guilt, despair, frustration or helplessness. Anger itself, especially at higher levels of intensity such as rage and fury, often incorporates a dual personality of its own that feeds on the very flames it fuels. Flames that enable us to lay blame anywhere except on ourselves.

Realize that you do have options to replace your angry reactions. Note: If you feel good enough about yourself, you can laugh or even agree with insults. If you feel bad about yourself, you may take them very, very seriously. You can select compassion, understanding (to know all is to forgive all), appreciation (you care enough about me to have deep feelings), pleasant acceptance, or humor, among other reactions.

Here are some examples:

EXAMPLE 1
You are driving home quietly, but impatiently, in heavy traffic. Someone suddenly speeds past you, cuts dangerously in front of you, and darts in and out among the other cars. You can choose any or all of the following "road rage" reactions: profuse profanity, giving the finger and boiling all the way home. Or you can choose reframing: maybe there's an emergency, and the driver is late getting there.

EXAMPLE 2
Your friend tells you that you are not only wrong in your opinion but that you are being loud, obnoxious and thoroughly disagreeable in your expression of it. Your choices: yell back at him or her in no uncertain language, stalk off, or terminate the friendship. Or reframing: could he or she possibly be right? Perhaps he or she is doing me a favor, and it takes courage to say those things to my face. Or maybe we're both just having bad hair days. Let's get away from each other and take it up again tomorrow when we're both calmer.

EXAMPLE 3
You have made a stupid mistake; there's no doubt about it; there's no one else to blame. It was stupid, stupid, stupid! Your choices: berate yourself, direct that insulting language at yourself; doubt your intelligence, your abilities, and yourself as a good person or try acceptance and gentle forgiveness. Perhaps there are even some legitimate excuses or reasons: I'm tired from working too hard; there's too much on my mind; nobody's perfect.

Often, we nurse anger by calling it righteous indignation; it helps us justify keeping our anger on ready reserve. Let pent-up anger go! Don't rehearse it over and over again. It hurts us more than it does the person with whom we are angry.

Become aware that anger can cover other emotions that are more difficult to accept, such as fear, anxiety, isolation, hurt, depression, loneliness, rejection, fatigue, shame, guilt, or diminishment. Take anger as a signal and an opportunity to examine yourself and your adversary.

If fear is the principal emotion underlying our anger, then, as Ralph Waldo Emerson (1909) told us, "Fear always springs from ignorance." Ignorance is not stupidity. Rather it is lacking some of the essential facts. *So the key is to let anger lead us to a deeper exploration of others and ourselves.* Better knowledge of one another can lead to greater intimacy and to a rediscovery of old feelings long smothered by blankets of anger. The Reverend Tom Conley told me, "I have found the more I understand an issue or a person, the less I am inclined to be angry." Mary MacQueen, Ph.D., told me also that in women, depression covers anger. In men, she said, anger covers depression; depression is often the result of anger turned inward because we feel we haven't "measured up" and can't or won't forgive ourselves.

When we learn more about ourselves and can begin to like and accept ourselves, we don't need to embrace anger. How to feel better about ourselves will be discussed in Chapter 4.

No one can make you angry unless you give him or her the power to do so. If you want to control your anger, you must first learn to control yourself!

Here is a personal experience. I had an old friend who was the chairman of a non-profit foundation. My son and I had invented and developed a software program called GOcabulary® to teach vocabulary and reading skills. This friend loved the program and suggested that his foundation could help in its further development and distribution. The foundation loved it too, and then my so-called friend and that foundation tried to steal it from us. He lied to us, to his own foundation, and to his greatest contributor.

His duplicitous actions, his condescending attitude, and his relentless efforts to pound us into submission drove both my son and me to distraction. I vowed never to speak to that traitor again. My wife Bettye, however, had a different perspective.

Several years later, my wife and I were having lunch at a downtown Atlanta restaurant. We saw this former friend a few tables away. She went over to speak to him. I did not. When she returned she said, "Darling, remember what you said about not choosing to hold on to your anger?" I realized that she was right. I went over and shook his hand, not warmly, but at least I made the effort. Sometime later, we met again. He told me how much that handshake had meant to him. I'm not angry anymore, but I still don't like him.

Anger sours, spoils and contaminates. Anger can turn

- Love to hate
- Happiness to sadness
- Peace to war
- Assertiveness to aggressiveness (including passive-aggressiveness)
- Discussion to argument
- Humor to sarcasm
- Kindness to cruelty
- Self-love to self-hate
- Productivity to destruction
- Suggestions to criticism
- Independence to defiance
- Appreciation to resentment
- Skepticism to cynicism

To summarize, *Breaking Anger's Embrace* will help you feel better about yourself, and feeling better about yourself will help you break anger's embrace. Simple enough? Go for it!

2
THE INVENTIVE ALTERNATIVES METHOD© FOR ELIMINATING "SELECTIVE" ANGER

As a clinical psychologist and couples and family therapist, I have long been intrigued with the intensely painful, pervasive, and extraordinarily complex phenomenon called anger. Over the years, I have developed some theories dealing with the elimination of anger in relationships—not anger management, nor anger reduction, but anger elimination, anger eradication, and anger extinction. Recently, Joan Thomas, a colleague of mine and a former journalist, asked me if these theories of mine could be applied to diminish "nationalized anger" resulting from the 9-11 trauma, other terrorist atrocities, the deaths of our service men and women in combat and through suicide, our increasingly challenging economy, the combative discourse promoted by hate-mongering extremists, xenophobia, racism, the inflammatory rhetoric of the politicians and their partisan supporters, and the failure of diplomatic negotiations in world-wide conflict resolution.

> "THE BETTER WE FEEL ABOUT OURSELVES, THE LESS WE NEED TO EMBRACE ANGER AS A RESPONSE."

What a challenge!

Since all of my hands-on experience has dealt primarily with clinical and organizational relationships and basic communication training, I can only present a hypothetical framework for application of these principles on a broader scale.

So, here are my theoretical building blocks:

1. Anger is an evolutionary survival emotion that prepares us to fight.

2. Anger is usually the initial primitive reaction to a situation in which we feel we have been hurt, wronged, diminished, attacked or insulted.

3. I say "usually" because on mature reflection we may realize that anger is not the only, but probably the worst, response available to us.

4. It is the "worst" response because anger, like other strong emotions, is highly contagious; and anger confronting anger only escalates to inflammatory proportions up to and including all out war.

5. Other, more sophisticated, healthier and productive options we may choose include compassion, understanding (to know all is to forgive all), appreciation (you care enough about me to feel deeply), pleasant acceptance, and humor.

6. Extended anger is the anger we "hang on to." It is physiologically, emotionally, and intellectually unhealthy to ourselves and to our relationships. So, why in the world do we choose to stay angry? Let's see.

    a. Anger can be a cover for other uncomfortable emotions that may be more difficult to accept, such as fear, anxiety, isolation, hurt, depression, loneliness, rejection, fatigue, shame, guilt or diminishment.

    b. We may actually *enjoy* holding onto our anger and calling it "resentment." By "bearing a grudge," we put the blame and responsibility on someone else. This superior attitude generates a feeling of "power." That power feels better to us than facing our other, less acceptable, underlying feelings.

    c. This stored-up anger can be used to energize motivations to attack the alleged perpetrators of the action that initially brought on our angry reactions, and the cycle continues.

7. Persuasive communication can never be successful in the presence of anger. Why not? Because as mentioned earlier, anger is the emotion that prepares us to fight not to change; and change is usually the goal of all persuasive communication. The difference between a discussion and an argument is that anger, which inhibits change, is always present in an argument; so, no one ever wins the argument—ever! Even when there are concessions on both sides, resentment will linger and, too often, sabotage future efforts toward reconciliation. (See Chapter 5.)

The next question then is how do we apply these principles toward solving problems and resolving conflicts?

My initial training as a couples and family therapist involved helping the participants find solutions, most of which involved some form of compromise. But, all too often, the result was unsatisfactory and did not last. In later years, I learned that if I could help them break the embrace of their anger, most couples and families were quite capable of solving their own problems with much more satisfactory results in both the long and short terms.

THE INVENTIVE ALTERNATIVE IS NOT A COMPROMISE. IT IS AN ENTIRELY NEW SOLUTION FORGED FROM THE COLLABORATIVE EFFORTS OF THE PARTICIPANTS IN ANY DISPUTE.

So, the major issue that remains is how to break anger's embrace. As stated before, this is not anger management, nor anger reduction, but *eliminating anger altogether*. So, I offer this new proposition: "The better we feel about ourselves the less we need to embrace anger as a response."

When we don't think well of ourselves, my major remedy is to discover, develop, use, and enjoy our own latent creativity. However, anger is such a potent and all-consuming emotion that it seldom allows us to focus on anything else, so our creativity remains buried under an avalanche of anger.

Breaking anger's embrace allows creativity to flow. So we engage in a reciprocal process: Breaking anger's embrace involves liberating creativity; liberating creativity involves breaking anger's embrace. See Chapter 4 for a detailed explanation about "uncorking your genie" and "liberating creativity."

This newly-liberated creativity can then be used to help resolve problems and conflicts and to break down communication barriers after the anger has gone. Then what happens? In my experience, this is where the concept of the **Inventive Alternative Method** comes in.

Note: For our purposes, creativity is originality in the arts. Inventiveness is originality in the sciences.

The inventive alternative method is not a compromise. It is an entirely new solution forged from the collaborative efforts of the participants in any dispute. The problem with compromise is that although it may be better than a standoff, it always leaves lingering dissatisfaction on both sides

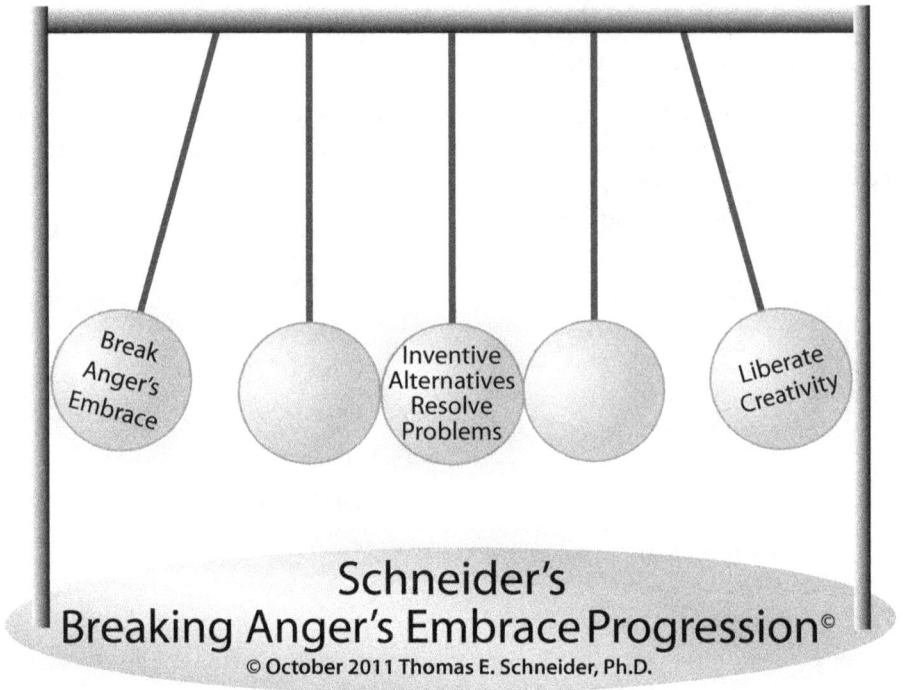

Schneider's
Breaking Anger's Embrace Progression©
© October 2011 Thomas E. Schneider, Ph.D.

which, like smoldering embers, may burst anew into angry flames. Also, compromise involves competition, grudging acquiescence, disappointment, and feelings of emptiness. Searching for inventive alternatives, on the other hand, invites and involves cooperation, sharing, enjoyment and fulfillment.

As the participants join the process of developing inventive alternatives, camaraderie may appear as pride replaces the real or perceived shame or weakness of concession. It is hoped that with pride comes increased self-confidence, greater self-esteem, and the consequent dissipation of anger. The energy that fed the anger and smothered creativity may now be directed toward the healing process.

Another observation on self-esteem: there are two sources through which we learn to feel good about ourselves. One is external when we receive love, acceptance, admiration and respect from others. The second is internal when we can take pride and feel fulfillment in being part of a creative process either individually or jointly.

Following are diagrammatic concepts of how this process takes place.

A. Why Compromise Fails

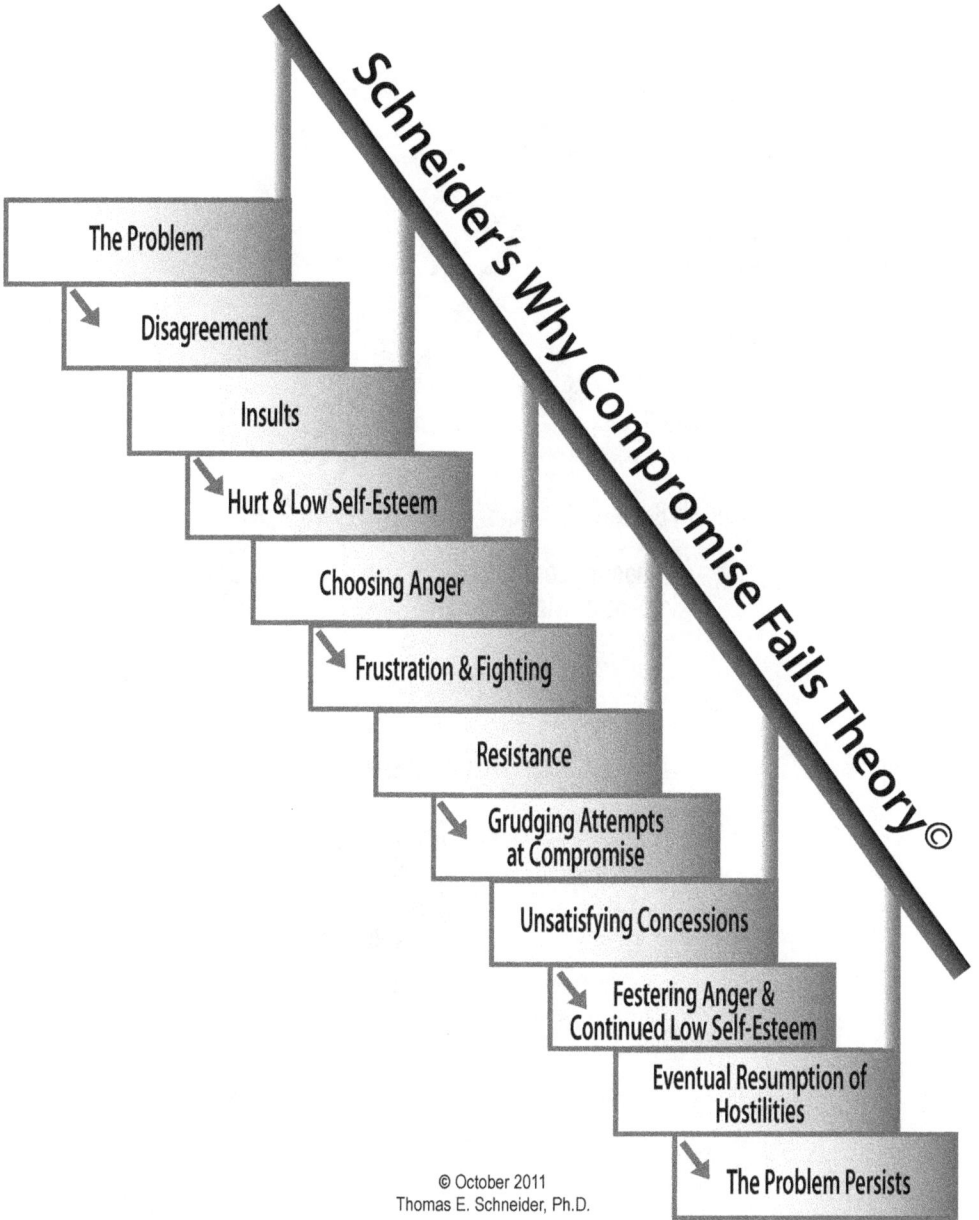

The Problem

Disagreement

Insults

Hurt & Low Self-Esteem

Choosing Anger

Frustration & Fighting

Resistance

Grudging Attempts at Compromise

Unsatisfying Concessions

Festering Anger & Continued Low Self-Esteem

Eventual Resumption of Hostilities

The Problem Persists

Schneider's Why Compromise Fails Theory©

© October 2011
Thomas E. Schneider, Ph.D.

B. Why Inventive Alternatives Succeed

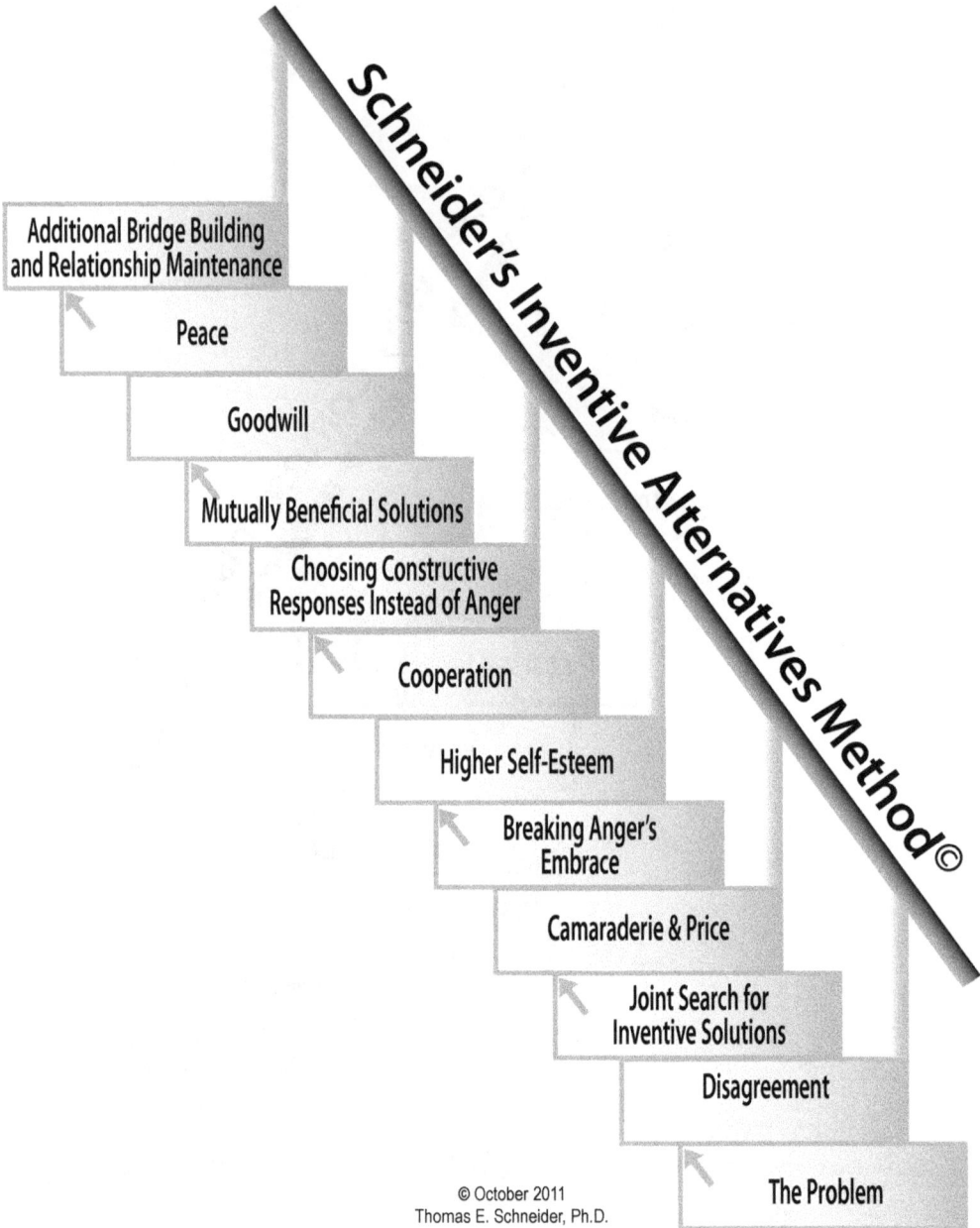

Schneider's Inventive Alternatives Method©

Additional Bridge Building and Relationship Maintenance

Peace

Goodwill

Mutually Beneficial Solutions

Choosing Constructive Responses Instead of Anger

Cooperation

Higher Self-Esteem

Breaking Anger's Embrace

Camaraderie & Price

Joint Search for Inventive Solutions

Disagreement

The Problem

© October 2011
Thomas E. Schneider, Ph.D.

Enough about theory! What about the practical aspects? How can these principles be put to work? Here are some potential applications to be submitted to negotiating committees:

1. **The proposed building of Islamic cultural centers in communities where some people may object.**

    Assemble scholars from Islam, Judaism, and Christianity to explore such possibilities as

    a. Constructing a center for the study of comparative religions

    b. Constructing a single house of worship and holding one, weekly, liturgical service prepared by the best clerical (religious) minds from the three major faiths

    c. Constructing a boarding school where young students from the three major faiths may live together and learn together the lessons from the Qur'an, the Torah, and the New Testament.

2. **Illegal Immigration**

    This one should be easy.

    a. In the case of the USA, instead of constructing endlessly futile and ridiculously expensive barriers along the southern border with Mexico, use that money to improve conditions for the people who would otherwise want to leave their homes and country for a better life in the USA.

    b. Work with neighboring governments and the international banking system to help the illegal migrants' countries build new communities with improved housing, health care, cleaner environments, and better schooling, and provide inventive incentives for developing new products and businesses there.

    c. Focus greater attention on employers who hire and sometimes exploit illegal workers. Work with those employers to establish legal ways to hire the labor they need at so-called "livable" wages that will still allow the employers to show a profit.

3. **Creation of an independent Palestinian state and the partitioning of Jerusalem**

    This may be the most difficult assignment of all, because the anger has run so deeply and lasted so long. However, the prospect of not trying and leaving things as they are is totally unacceptable. The needless taking of even one more life due to cultural and theological differences is egregiously unconscionable, immoral and ineffective, especially since there are always inventive alternatives just waiting to be discovered.

IT IS HOPED THAT WITH PRIDE COMES INCREASED SELF-CONFIDENCE, GREATER SELF-ESTEEM, AND THE CONSEQUENT DISSIPATION OF ANGER. THE ENERGY THAT FED THE ANGER AND SMOTHERED CREATIVITY MAY NOW BE DIRECTED TOWARD THE HEALING PROCESS.

a. Assemble a strongly-motivated team of envoys and negotiators and train them in facilitating the principles of *Breaking Anger's Embrace,* and put them to work immediately.

b. Among the participants must be Palestinians, Israelis, Jordanians, Egyptians, Lebanese, Syrians, Iranians, Turks, Europeans and Americans.

4. **Burning copies of the Qur'an**

The (literally) inflammatory, vindictive nature of this idea, this threat, this act—which can only intensify latent anger and invite retaliation—is so obtusely offensive and totally un-Christian (love your enemies?) that the only possible inventive alternative that I can think of is to ask the provocateurs to put their ideology on trial and to judge it using the words of Jesus Christ whom they claim to love.

a. One inventive alternative to counter the destructive philosophies of extremist Muslims is to stop fearing all Muslims and identify and reject the real enemies of peace.

b. Another inventive alternative would be to work with moderate Muslims to bridge religious and cultural divides.

TIPS FOR IMPLEMENTING THE INVENTIVE ALTERNATIVES METHOD© IN NEGOTIATING GROUPS:

1. **The Warm-Up**

Even though this proposal is likely to be met with resistance, scorn or disbelief, plunge ahead and urge a demonstration of intellectual flexibility. Before serious negotiating sessions, let participants warm up together with games such as the following:

a. Employ the yoga tactic of standing in a circle and playing catch with a tennis ball, followed by discussion about who made the most catches and why. For example, if participants tended to throw the ball to one person more than the others how does that recipient feel? Also, how do the other participants feel about not being favored in that way?

> THE PURPOSE OF THE WARM-UP EXERCISES IS TO "GROUND" THE PARTICIPANTS TO BRING THEM "DOWN TO EARTH" AND TO GIVE THEM THE UNIQUE EXPERIENCE OF GETTING TO KNOW ONE ANOTHER THROUGH PLAY AND COOPERATIVE CREATIVITY.

b. Participants are asked to sit on the floor in a circle, as close to one another as possible without touching. Their assignment is to pass a tennis ball around the circle while the facilitator plays music. No one may throw the ball; anyone who drops the ball must leave the circle. When the music stops (at the discretion of the facilitator) whoever is holding the ball must leave the circle. The last person left is declared the winner. Discussion follows about the experience.

c. Compose, jointly, a song for peace among people and nations. Write new sets of lyrics to mutually familiar tunes. The song could have three verses. One verse could be in Arabic, another in Hebrew and the third in English, and the song should be learned by the participants.

If all goes well, and the exercises are enjoyable, it will be time to proceed with the serious negotiations. If, however, hostility is apparent, it may be wise to postpone the meeting until emotions are settled and under amicable control.

Does this approach sound silly or childish? I've seen it work wonders with businesses and other organizational groups. Isn't it worth a try?

2. Preparation of the Groups

Now, these proposed solutions are merely the musings of an inventive lay person. Think what a group of experts might do if they succeeded in *breaking anger's embrace* and allowed their creative juices to flow!

The purpose of the warm-up exercises is to "ground" the participants to bring them "down to earth" and to give them the unique experience of getting to know one another through play and cooperative creativity. More than 170 years ago, Ralph Waldo Emerson wrote that "fear always springs from ignorance." I agree with him and believe fear is beneath most of our anger; and beneath the fear lies ignorance, not stupidity but rather a lack of information, knowledge about those with whom we disagree and facts about their opinions and positions.

So before beginning our exercises and sessions, we must ask our participants to learn all they can about one another: personal, professional and political identities.

3. **Composition of the Groups**

In Western culture, the number **three**, throughout the ages, has proven to be a magic number.

- Mother, Father and Child
- The Three Bears
- The Three Blind Mice
- The Three Wise Men
- The Three Angles on a Pyramid
- The Holy Trinity

So, I propose using "three" as the basic unit structure for the Inventive Alternatives Method©.

Politicians	Clerics	Pundits
Representative 1	Imam 1	Pundit 1
Representative 2	Rabbi 2	Pundit 2
Representative 3	Cleric 3	Pundit 3

Can't you just picture these distinguished dignitaries sitting on the floor (with carpets of course—preferably magic), thinking, creating, playing and enjoying the interaction with one another? If there are too many participants for this to be practical, each group may want to appoint a spokesperson to do the physical work while the other two act as advisors.

4. Schedules (one-day program)

Time	Activities
08:00	Eat breakfast together with members of the same discipline
09:30	Begin the three exercises with members of all disciplines: tennis balls; songs
12:00	Eat a light lunch, with no alcohol, with members of another discipline where possible
13:00	Begin deliberations on "Inventive Alternatives"
15:00	Refreshment Break
15:30	Resume deliberations on "Inventive Alternatives"
17:00	End deliberations
17:30–18:30	Break/Naps
19:00	Eat an evening meal (seated at will; still no alcohol; perhaps serving delicacies from each ethnic cuisine while observing religious customs regarding the type and preparation of food)
20:00	Sum up; write and submit reports
21:00	Conclusions & Commitments: ◆ Pledge to put into practice "Inventive Alternatives" that have been identified and accepted during the gathering. ◆ Confirm preliminary timelines and schedule follow-up meetings.
22:00	Recreation and farewells (literally)

NOTE:

Until the entire program has been completed, the following rules will apply:

◆ No Reporters   ◆ No Photos

◆ No Recordings   ◆ No Smart Phones

◆ No Interruptions ◆ No Computers

◆ No Radio/TV   ◆ No Visitors

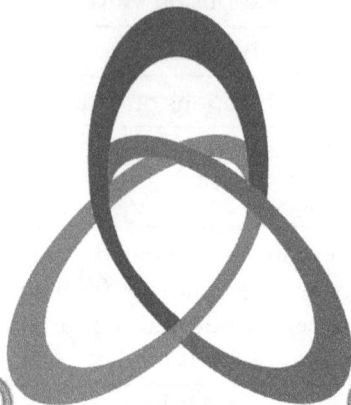

Peace Whorl[©]

Shalom

Peace

Salaam

© October 2011
Thomas E. Schneider, Ph.D.

3
AN INVENTIVE ALTERNATIVE TO ANGER MANAGEMENT

While anger management does not have a particularly good track record, it has been useful with certain populations.

However, my concern, based on my clinical experience, is that managing, controlling, or reducing anger, while often helpful, is simply not enough. What is needed is to eliminate the anger altogether. Here's what I propose:

PRINCIPLES FOR BREAKING ANGER'S EMBRACE

I am convinced there is a significant difference between anger management and what I call, "breaking anger's embrace." "Anger management" implies learning to control the anger that you hang onto. Breaking anger's embrace means letting go of that anger altogether. Let's examine this further:

DEFINITIONS OF ANGER

A. Anger and Change

1. Anger is an emotion that energizes fighting not changing.

2. The difference between a discussion and an argument is the presence of anger in the latter.

3. The goal of most serious discussions is to effect change; but, when anger is present, the mood is combative not cooperative.

4. Change that is forced through duress seldom lasts.

5. Anger is contagious; so an angry assertion usually invites an angry reaction.

B. Anger and Choice

   1. Holding onto anger is our own choice and our own responsibility. No one can "make you angry" just as no one can "make you happy." Holding onto anger is unhealthy for us and our relationships.

   2. Other more sophisticated, healthier and productive options we may choose include compassion, understanding, curiosity, pleasant acceptance and humor

   3. We hang onto our anger because it can act as a cover for other uncomfortable emotions that may be more difficult to accept, such as fear, anxiety, isolation, hurt, depression, loneliness, rejection, fatigue, shame, guilt or diminishment.

   4. Anger can make us feel powerful (at least temporarily), as it allows us to shift the blame to others.

C. Anger and Creativity

   1. The better we feel about ourselves, the less we need to embrace anger as a response.

   2. Feeling better about ourselves involves receiving approval from ourselves and others. We can achieve this by releasing our latent creativity to benefit ourselves and others. (See Chapter 4.)

   3. Unfortunately, anger is such a potent and all-consuming emotion that it will seldom allow us to focus on anything else; our creativity remains buried under an avalanche of anger. "Breaking anger's embrace" then allows our creativity to flow so we can engage in a reciprocal process: "Breaking anger's embrace" involves liberating creativity; liberating creativity involves "breaking anger's embrace."

D. Problem-Solving and Conflict Resolution

   1. Participants collaborate in finding and implementing INVENTIVE ALTERNATIVES.

   2. The inventive alternative is not a compromise. It is an entirely new solution forged from the collaborative efforts of the participants in any dispute.

3. The problem with compromise is that, although it may be better than a standoff, it always leaves lingering dissatisfaction on both sides which, like smoldering embers, may at any time burst anew into angry flames.

4. Compromise involves competition, grudging acquiescence, disappointment, and feelings of emptiness. Searching for inventive alternatives, on the other hand, invites and involves cooperation, sharing, enjoyment and fulfillment.

5. Participants working together on "Inventive Alternatives" have an opportunity to reinforce one another's self-esteem—one more building block in eliminating their anger.

6. The only way to solve systems' (families, groups, organizations, etc.) conflicts is for all participants to have equal power and for all participants to stop posturing and playing political games that don't promote the common good. Multiple problems must be dealt with one at a time: separate and simplify.

EXAMPLE: A SUCCESSFUL INVENTIVE ALTERNATIVE

An affluent Chinese couple had homes and businesses in both Shanghai and Atlanta. Their two young children had been attending private schools while alternating between the two cities. The father wanted the children to return to school in Shanghai, but the mother and the children wanted to remain in Atlanta. This led to a lot of arguing, crying, and anger.

I suggested that the decision was not as important as the process of making that decision and that their assignment was to agree on an inventive alternative. They did, and the Atlanta school agreed on a plan under which the children would attend school in Shanghai where they would act as the Atlanta school's correspondents.

The family was delighted with the plan to set up a conference call with the children's classmates each Friday during which they would report on their week's activities in China. There were no more hassles, no more arguing, no more anger, just one satisfied family who had joined the supporters of inventive alternatives.

4
THE ANCESTRAL UNCONSCIOUS: UNCORKING YOUR GENIE

In many ways, this has been the most difficult chapter for me to compose; particularly because I believe this to be the most important insight of all. To find suitable symbols, metaphors, or analogies to express abstract concepts in concrete terms is always a challenge for an author. I have wrestled to find ways of describing genie, *under-conscious, ancestral unconscious,* and *shadow cork.* Finally, in the midst of these struggles, it dawned on me to try practicing what I was preaching and call on my own genie for help. Here is what the genie and I uncorked.

Embracing or not embracing anger as our response to a given situation is usually a function of our mood. The worse our mood, the more likely we are to select an angry response. Our moods are products of chemical balance and/or how we feel about ourselves. Here's a new proposition to build on:

The better we feel about ourselves, the less we need to embrace anger as a response.

If you have chosen to stay angry, ask yourself, "Why is it that I'm not pleased with myself? How do I go about feeling better about me?" Instead of contemplating, "What is the meaning of life?" it may be more useful to ask, "What can give meaning to my life? Am I a generative (inventive and contributing) person? If not, how do I become one?" The answers, I believe, lie inside each of us.

> THE ANCESTRAL UNCONSCIOUS IS NOT SOME INEXPLICABLE PHENOMENON. IT IS PRESENT IN OUR GENES AS A VAST LEGACY FROM OUR ANCESTORS ...

How do we go about finding what or who is in there? Let's begin with the mind. Psychologists and psychiatrists picture the self as having two levels: conscious, and unconscious or subconscious. Swiss psychiatrist C.G. Jung posited another type of unconscious presence. He called it the "collective unconscious." Jung believed that this was the part of the psyche that held humanity's join psychological inheritance. Therein, he believed, lie memories, knowledge, and truths that are common to all beings. The French philosopher René Descartes called these "eternal verities;" Jung called them "archetypes", a term first used by Plato. In *Man and His Symbols* (1985), Jung defined them as "archaic remnants" or "primordial images", universal myths. Maybe there is even more to the story.

Current brain research indicates that long-term memories are stored in the lower regions of the hippocampus, a part of the limbic system of the brain.

Perhaps in addition to conscious and unconscious memory, there is a third level. Let's call it the *"under-conscious."*

The first level is that of the conscious mind, the part of ourselves of which we are most aware during our waking hours.

The second or unconscious level stays on the fringe, may occasionally come into our waking awareness, and is most conspicuous through our dreams or in prayer or meditation. This level contains thoughts, feelings, and memories of which we may not be aware and which may cause us to behave in ways that we do not understand.

The third level, the "under-conscious," has, as I have experienced it, two components: Jung's "collective unconscious" and a companion one, which I call our "ancestral unconscious." While the collective unconscious contains memories common to all of us (archetypes), the ancestral unconscious is composed of memories, skills, and traits, specific to the individual. Let's call them "ideotypes."

Why don't most of us have access to these attributes? If we did, perhaps we would feel better about who and what we are and be able to use these qualities to benefit ourselves and others. How do we get to them?

The ancestral unconscious is not some inexplicable phenomenon. It is present in our genes as a vast legacy from our ancestors, passed on from generation to generation just as are our physical and emotional characteristics, our intelligence, interests, and instincts. This unrealized knowledge is too often held in check by our anger and other strong emotions such as fear or depression and often by less dramatic but equally insidious impediments such as indifference, boredom, or just plain laziness. Albert Einstein (1956) said, "Imagination is more important than knowledge." We may not all have the same capacity to acquire knowledge, but we have all been blessed with the ability to imagine. It is, therefore, our imagination that may be trapped under all these negative emotions.

Picture your lower hippocampus as a bottle with a cork in it, a "shadow cork." This cork is actually a compressed mass of those debilitating, negative emotions, glued together by anger. The cork blocks access to and egress from our ancestral unconscious. How do we dissolve or extract this shadow cork?

This is where our marvelous genie comes in. There, dormant at the bottom of our hippocampus, lie all those positive but unrecognized attributes (ideotypes) trapped by that inhibiting shadow cork, unable to move, with no means of release.

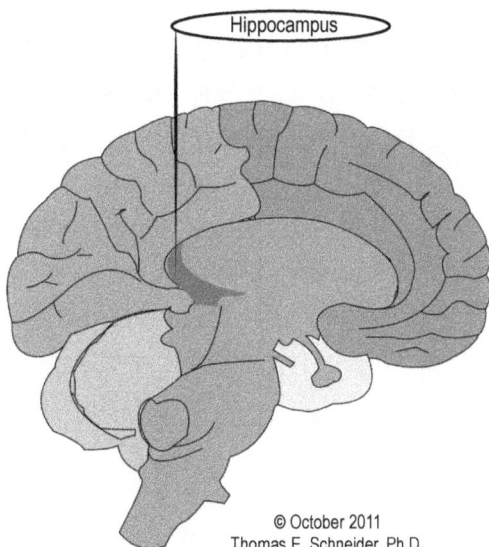

Hippocampus

© October 2011
Thomas E. Schneider, Ph.D.

To follow this part, you must be willing to accept the concept of "spirits." These spirits are not some ephemeral fantasies but are actual presences capable of being experienced by all of us. Examples are the Great Spirit of the Native Americans, the Holy Spirit of numerous religions, and the human spirit present in all persons.

In addition, I have found another spiritual presence, perhaps an offspring of the others, but unique to each individual. This is the one I call our genie. This genie is often trapped in our hippocampal bottle along with the other denizens of our ancestral unconscious.

Our genie's first function is to pick away at the cork from below. When it starts to crumble, the genie gathers our escaping attributes, conveying them to conscious awareness. Its second function is to act as the spiritual transmitter for these attributes, so we can hear what the attributes are trying to tell us. The genie can't do it all on its own; it needs our help cutting away at the top of the cork, while it breaks through from the bottom like partners on a cross-cut saw. How? The first step is choosing not to hold on to anger. That means breaking anger's embrace!

Giving up the anger provides moments of calm, which enable us to listen to the voice of our genie. Just listen. No prayer, no contemplation; just be silent and listen and look with William Wordsworth's inward eye "which is the bliss of solitude." It will come to you. Perhaps all inspiration is divine, and we just don't recognize it. Clear your mind and wait. It's not an easy task. But that's where inspiration and revelation lie. They have been waiting there all along. So, that's the ticket: *Uncork your genie to liberate your creativity.*

LET THE POTENTIALS IN SILENCE OVERCOME THE POWER OF ANGER. IN THAT SILENCE YOU MAY NOT ONLY FIND YOURSELF BUT ALSO "THE PEACE THAT PASSETH UNDERSTANDING ..." (PHILIPPIANS 4:7)

Now, in the unlikely event that no special personal talent comes to mind at first, perhaps your genie needs a little help. So, if you can, research your ancestors to see what talents they may have possessed. You may find something just for you. I like to call this search your "genie-ology". Okay, maybe it's a bad pun, but I hope it makes the point.

As you liberate these qualities and begin to use them, you will begin to feel better about yourself and will lose your need to cling to your anger. If you feel good enough about yourself, you can laugh at, or even agree with, real or perceived insults. Let the potentials in silence overcome the power of anger. In that silence you may not only find yourself but also "the peace that passeth understanding ..." (Philippians 4:7).

Pursue happiness. You might want to consider first uncorking your genie, and then let it help you find that bliss. *That's the key: liberate and listen!* If you liberate your genie now, the possibilities are endless.

I have come to realize that the road to and fulfillment has two lanes. Let's call them "creativity" and "contribution." Creativity is a process realized with the help of our genie. We discover it within ourselves and then produce something of value that is exclusively ours. It doesn't matter what it is. It could be a poem, a prayer, the great American novel, a collection of life experiences, a song, a ship in a bottle, a piece of sculpture, a picture, a dance, planting a garden, or any of dozens of possible creations. It is only necessary to enjoy the process and enrich oneself.

The second part that I call "contribution" means giving of oneself to someone else. Contribution can be of special merit when the self feels fulfilled. The parts given away will be of greater value. Money or material wealth although very helpful, does not give the same rich feeling of self-worth. Contribution requires your personal touch. Serving on boards, giving of time—while useful—doesn't do it either. Contribution must be a gift of self.

What is a gift of self? Formally adopt a child, teach someone to read, become a mentor, feed the hungry, visit a prisoner, or care for the sick or lonely. It may sound trite, but when we do these things, we receive a great deal more than we give. We might label it "selfish unselfishness," and that is fulfillment!

Creativity can bring personal joy and contribution can bring joy to others.

Share joy!

5
PERSUASIVE COMMUNICATION: LISTEN MORE, TALK LESS

By persuasive communication, I mean conversations where change is the goal. Such conversations usually require both participants to deal with feelings. As stated in Chapter 3, the key to the successful exchange of ideas is the absence of anger. Why? Because when we are angry, we want to fight not change. Even if we realize that our adversary is right, we will still resist.

If and when anger is no longer present, the next step toward being a successful communicator is to cultivate the power of empathic listening. There are numerous classes in public speaking but few in private listening. Successful communication depends on the ability to *listen*. People pay professionals a great deal of money just to be *heard*. It is possible to learn to listen just as trained counselors do. Here are some guidelines for developing the healing power of listening:

PAY ATTENTION TO TIMING
Pick a time when both participants are not rushed. Use a reasonably quiet and secluded place. Make sure neither person is angry. Remember, the difference between an argument and a discussion is the presence or absence of anger. Nobody ever wins an argument! Do not drink alcohol before or during your conversation. Drinking is for relaxation, not serious business. Drinking alters the mind.

CHECK ATTITUDES AND FEELINGS
Are you angry, anxious, or depressed? Are you accepting and respectful? Do you want to be helpful or controlling? Whose best interest do you have at heart? Would you be willing to change if you were in the other person's seat listening to you?

LISTEN NON-DEFENSIVELY

Are you trying to protect your own viewpoint? Being right is not all that important and may only serve to put down the other person. If you are right, then the other person must be wrong. Put-downs cause hurt feelings that lead to anger. We know the damage that can cause. The need to be right is always a function of insecurity, so the better you feel about yourself, the less need you will have to be right.

It is important to be aware that we are always more approachable when we are vulnerable (able to admit that we are wrong) than when we are invincible (never wrong).

REMEMBER, BEING KIND IS ALWAYS MORE IMPORTANT THAN BEING RIGHT.

LISTEN NON-JUDGMENTALLY

Are you injecting your own value system instead of trying to understand the other person?

REFRAIN FROM OFFERING A SOLUTION

Do you trust other people to come up with their own answers to their own problems?

SUMMARIZE OR PARAPHRASE

Can you reflect what the other person has said using your own words without interposing your point of view?

DON'T CRITICIZE JUDGMENTALLY

Remember, criticism usually brings on anger. Anger promotes resistance, anger is contagious; we don't change when we are angry.

DON'T INTERRUPT

Keep the conversations going! Let others have their full say. Use conversational lubricants such as: "Hmm, I see. Oh, that's interesting. Tell me more. That sounds important. How do you feel about _____? (Fill in the blank.)

LISTEN FOR THE FEELINGS BEHIND THE WORDS

Do you recognize that all feelings are legitimate? There is no such thing as a right or wrong feeling, only right or wrong behaviors. Can you reflect the other person's feelings? For example, "That sounds painful" or "I can sense your sadness."

ALLOW INDIVIDUALS TO EXPRESS THEIR ANGRY FEELINGS WITHOUT BECOMING ANGRY YOURSELF

Can you tell people that you are angry about their behavior without attacking their personality or character? Can your anger be expressed in non-destructive ways?

AVOID GENERALIZING

"You always" and "you never" are never true and always inflammatory.

THE BEST LISTENERS ASK QUESTIONS RATHER THAN MAKE STATEMENTS

For example, someone says, "We just got back from a wonderful trip to New York." The good listener says, "Oh, sounds like fun. What did you do?" The bad listener says, "Oh, we went to New York last year, and this is what we did."

THE MOST IMPORTANT SUGGESTION OF ALL

The healing power of listening is often achieved when we say nothing but are simply there.

When you do talk, try to follow these suggestions. And, again, check your *attitude* and *feelings*. Is anger present?

1. *Be specific.* Remember that there is a difference between fact and opinion. While all of us have a right to our own opinions, facts are harder to deny. Use examples and data to support your facts. Be Brief!

2. *Use checkpoints.* Take a breath. Ask for feedback.

   What did you hear me say?" Better one sentence understood than a page wasted. When we talk in lengthy paragraphs, our listeners forget by the end what we said at the beginning. Try speaking just one sentence at a time. *Keep it short!*

3. *Don't monopolize.* Speeches are for the podium, sermons for the pulpit, and lectures for the classroom. People who talk constantly are rude, self-centered, and boring. They assume that what they say is more important than what their listeners have to say. They are usually wrong and often obnoxious. Have you noticed that people who talk too much are usually anxious when they are not in control? They have never learned to appreciate the sacredness of silence.

REMEMBER THE WORDS OF THE SAGE WHO SAID,
"NEVER BREAK A SILENCE UNLESS YOU CAN IMPROVE IT."

4. *Don't send solutions.* Try to avoid ordering, advising, or exhorting. As Oscar Wilde observed, "It is always a silly thing to give advice, but to give good advice is absolutely fatal." Why? Sending solutions promotes resistance. It also implies that other people can't find their own solutions; they usually can if their anger is dissipated (Chapter 3).

5. *Use "I" messages rather than "You" messages.* Doing so helps us accept responsibility for our feelings. For example, "I feel uncomfortable when we start raising our voices." These messages are less likely to cause resistance and rebellion because they are not usually threatening. "You" messages, on the other hand, usually are accusatory and put the listener on the defensive. For example, "You always yell at me" or "You never let me say anything."

FINALLY, REMEMBER, PEOPLE DON'T USUALLY CHANGE WHEN THEY ARE TALKED TO, BUT THEY MAY CHANGE IF THEY FEEL THEY ARE BEING HEARD.

6
PREMARITAL COUNSELING

Several years ago, an Episcopal priest asked me to help him prepare a program for premarital counseling.

As my training had taught me, I undertook a literature review. Internet search engines and vendors displayed more than 1,500 books on the subject and listed almost 70 journal articles. That bounty was more than I had bargained for, so I turned to three experienced colleagues with years of work in the premarital counseling field: the Reverend Tom Conley, an Episcopal priest and psychotherapist, Mary MacQueen, Ph.D., who has conducted numerous group programs for the diocese of Atlanta, and the Reverend Dr. Bill Harkins, another priest and therapist.

> **NEVER CRITICIZE JUDGMENTALLY, NEVER TRY TO CHANGE YOUR PARTNER, AND NEVER TRY TO PERSUADE. YOU CAN ONLY CHANGE YOURSELF, AND THAT IS NEVER EASY.**

In addition to providing me with their own views, they recommended that I investigate the work of three authors: Charles W. Taylor, Philip Culbertson, David and Amy Olson.

These distinguished authors agree in many areas. I have tried in my own list of suggestions to make sure that I have paid respect to their views.

From a clinical perspective I will list below what I have found to be the most persistent problems confronting the dysfunctional couples I have worked with over the years. Then I will give suggestions for remedies that have been useful. Finally, I will put together a composite program that includes some of what I have learned from my research as well as techniques of my own that are designed to help new couples avoid these pitfalls. It's a big task, but here goes:

Anger, anger, anger: In my experience, this insidious emotion underlies 90 percent of couples' problems. I try to teach them how to eliminate this hazardous obstacle. If successful, they can usually solve the rest of their problems on their own (see Chapters 3, 4, and 6).

Sexual issues: "The thrill has gone." Anger, once again, is usually present here. If anger is removed, the partners can focus on getting to know each other all over again, remain faithful, and discover their "spiritual sexuality" (see Chapter 9).

Children and discipline: The couple must agree on methods of child rearing and on not putting children above a partner (see Chapter 8).

Family of origin issues: I agree completely with the experts: partners must come first. Period! No exceptions! Ever!

Finances: The love of money may not be the root of all evil, but disagreements over it can cause a cascade of troubles. My suggestions: Agree upfront on a budget and stick to it. Keep separate bank accounts. Consider homemaking to be an important occupation. It is just as valuable as any other job. Pay the homemaker a fair salary so he or she never has to ask for money, which can be a humiliating experience.

Control and decision-making: Who has the most power in the relationship? Do the individuals treat each other with dignity and respect? If contempt is present, troubles follow.

Criticism and change: Never criticize judgmentally, never try to change your partner, and never try to persuade. You can only change yourself, and that is never easy.

Chores: Decide ahead of time who will be responsible for what duties, and stick to it. Both partners should share the responsibilities.

Arguments: Here comes that old nemesis anger again. No one ever wins an argument. Get rid of the anger and productive discussions can follow.

Alcohol: Boy, is this a problem! Countless couples are beset and besieged with problems caused by alcohol consumption. So, it is very, very, very important to explore views on drinking, right at the beginning.

Here's one example out of many:

I worked with a married couple a few years ago. The husband was a teetotaler but had no objections to his wife having a glass of wine or two after a hard day's work to relax before dinner. Over time, the "glass or two" kept increasing until the husband became worried when his wife had reached a bottle a night. Her response to his expression of concern was, "I need it to relax." Sadly, their marriage ended in divorce.

If you believe you need alcohol to relax or to enjoy yourself, you may find all too soon that you are hooked. I think it wise to consider these consequences before you treat alcohol casually.

Values: spiritual, moral, economic, and social: Find out ahead of time where you both stand on each of these issues. Do you share the same beliefs? If not, would you be willing to change your views in order to form a more perfect union? What are your priorities? It is better to try working out differences ahead of time than after it is too late.

Moods: Disposition is a tremendously important and little considered factor in premarital counseling. Is either party moody? Does he or she pout? Where does he or she stand on acceptance and/or forgiveness? Does your partner bear grudges? Is either person chronically angry, depressed, or anxious? Is your partner currently taking or willing to take medications for any of these conditions? If both partners have cheerful temperaments, the chances for long-term compatibility are excellent. If not, trouble may lie ahead.

Now I realize that this is a lot of material to cover in a short time. At the time this book was being written, the Episcopal Diocese of Atlanta required six premarital counseling sessions; but, because the content is left to the individual counselors, there is no uniform procedure.

Here are my suggestions regarding premarital counseling in general:

SESSION 1: INITIAL INTERVIEWING
I don't use personality tests for several reasons. First, they take too much time for the value received. Second, their statistical properties are highly suspect. The best statistician I know told me he would place the most popular of these tests right up there with parlor games. Third, there is little predictive validity regarding which personality types are most compatible or incompatible.

What I recommend then is that each person be asked ahead of time to write a brief autobiographical sketch and mail it to the counselor prior to the initial interview. Then I ask about any issues related to the families of origin or foster parents. How did and do the individuals get along with their biological or surrogate parents? What did they learn from them about raising children, resolving conflicts, making decisions, handling secrets, sex, and affection? More simply put, how were they raised?

Moving to the present, I ask what they like and dislike about each other, what they appreciate and what they resent, what they would change, what are their expectations, and how do they handle conflicts now?

SESSION 2: EMOTIONS AND MOODS
I suggest for this session that the counselor explore both individuals' histories of moods, especially the issues of fragility, handling hurt feelings, and tendencies to hold onto and obsess over past hurts. Next, I recommend talking about anger elimination and improving self-esteem. These are covered in depth in Chapters 2, 3 and 4. If the couple can learn to cope with anger and use these methods to build each other's self-esteem, then they can head off a great deal of future trouble.

SESSION 3: RULES AND EXPECTATIONS
This session should deal with the issues of money, chores, child rearing, alcohol or drug use, and sex.

SESSION 4: POWER, CONTROL AND COMMUNICATION
In this session I recommend covering the items of decision making without arguments, using "I" rather than "you" messages (Chapter 5) and, finally, treating each other with dignity and respect rather than criticism and contempt.

If during these four sessions the counselor finds reasons to delay the wedding, these should be discussed, recommendations (e.g. couples therapy) made, and sessions 5 and 6 delayed.

SESSIONS 5 AND 6: RELIGION, SPIRITUALITY AND TRADITIONS
These should focus on religion, spiritual goals, and the marriage ceremony itself. If the couple (and counselor) can survive this rigorous program with affection, appreciation, and determination, the chances for a successful marriage should be excellent. God bless them all!

7
THERAPY FOR COUPLES

I wrote my first draft of this essay several years ago, basing it on my experiences as a couples and family therapist. Since that time I have studied extensively the work and theories of two of the foremost researchers in the marital therapy field: John M. Gottman, Ph.D., (1999) and Leslie S. Greenberg, Ph.D., (2008).

These two distinguished and brilliant social scientists differ in their theoretical approaches and techniques. Gottman's views are primarily cognitive-behavioral and Greenberg's are emotion-focused. Many of their conclusions and recommendations are, nevertheless, similar. My own experiential and intuitive methods both differ from and concur with them. I tip my hat to them. My own theories and techniques, as expressed in my original essay, are summarized as follows:

> **ALL TOO OFTEN I HEAR FROM COUPLES THAT THEY HAVE "FALLEN OUT OF LOVE."**

1. Get rid of anger (on both sides), and the couple is then perfectly able to solve most of their own problems and resolve their own conflicts. As stated in Chapter 1, breaking anger's embrace, not anger management, is the goal.

2. When anger is gone, the couple can work on the communicative guidelines suggested in Chapter 5.

3. Spoil each other generously every day.

4. Always discuss; never argue. When and if discussion turns to argument, as it always does when anger is present, stop, back off, and let the anger dissipate. And never discuss anything important when you are drinking.

5. Always praise; never criticize. Negative criticism is seldom well-received.

6. Always say what you mean; never use sarcasm. Sarcasm always hurts, and hurt causes resentment.

7. Always appreciate; never complain. Complaining and nagging never produce positive results; they just make things worse.

8. Keep in touch, every day. Hold hands, hug, pat, stroke, or kiss. *Never underestimate the power of touching!* When a couple that I am seeing in therapy has a heated argument, I often ask them to stop, hold hands and then continue. The changes in the emotional atmosphere are usually palpable.

9. Never "have sex;" always "make love."

10. Always speak softly; never yell. Yelling degrades both the speaker and the listener.

11. Always affirm; never correct. Correcting implies that you know what's right for the other person. You don't!

12. Always be dependable; never make promises you cannot keep. Trust is built by what is done, not by what is said.

13. Be realistic about your partner. We seldom live up to false expectations.

14. Hang in there; be persistent. Don't think (or threaten) about leaving when things go wrong.

15. Remain faithful. All too often I hear from couples that they have fallen out of love. How do they get that "in love" feeling back? I have two thoughts that I have found to be helpful:

    a. First, my wonderful old mentor, John Warkinton, used to tell me that the original "in love" feeling never leaves us; it just gets covered over and buried under negative feelings accumulated over the years. If John was right, and I think he was, then the principal culprit for smothering emotion is, without a doubt, anger. So the methods discussed in Chapters 3 and 4 may be employed to help release the couples' original feelings, along with their personal "genies."

    b. Second, discovering spiritual sexuality can be an exciting and rewarding pursuit. Getting to know your partner at a level deeper than the carnal façade can lead to a caring union that lasts long after the original allure has lost its glamour.

16. Keep separate bank accounts. If a spouse or domestic partner is not working outside the home, he or she should receive earned income, not an allowance. Homemaking is just as demanding and necessary as commercial work and should be respected and compensated as such.

17. Share and practice spiritual values together. "If God does not build the house, the builders work in vain" (Psalm 127:1)

18. Say, "I love you" often.

19. "Share joy" often.

20. Memorize this and include it among your regular prayers or meditations:

> *One day when I'm perfect and wondrously wise,*
>
> *I may give advice and perhaps criticize.*
>
> *But till that day comes,*
>
> *And it may take a while,*
>
> *Help me practice acceptance and polish my smile.*

One important factor that neither Gottman nor Greenberg presents is mood. If the prevailing wind in one partner or the other is cheerful, the chances are that life for both can be rosy. If there are winds of hostility, depression or anxiety, storms will invariably follow. Medications and psychotherapy for these conditions have advanced markedly in recent years, and what a difference they can make.

Another factor with which I continue to struggle is an understanding of the concept of forgiveness. I have a nagging feeling that forgiveness is too tied in with righteousness and carries a holier-than-thou sort of condescension: *"I am right; you are wrong, but in my graciousness, I forgive you. But you should still feel ashamed, and don't let it happen again."* Gentle acceptance, on the other hand, gets away from the one-up, one-down position, eases the burden of shame, and can lead to reconciliation free from guilt. I still don't have a firm grip on all this, but I continue to think about it.

8
PRACTICALLY PERFECT PARENTING

Is this yet another treatise advising parents on how to raise their bewildering offspring? Surely there are enough suggestions and enough advice for everyone from a variety of sources.

Why are there so many opinions and so much variance? The answer is that many acknowledged experts do not agree. The same is true of legions of parents.

Some of the parents with whom I have worked over the years subscribe to the old adage, "Spare the rod and spoil the child." Others consider punishment cruel. They don't use it at all. Although both of these approaches are sometimes successful, in most instances neither is. Why?

Systematically punished children too often grow up angry and resentful. Undisciplined children can turn into obnoxious brats. So what are new parents to do? What expert should they believe? Let's try me! As a parent, grandparent—lately a great grandparent—and family therapist for more than 40 years, I have a few very specific ideas that I hope you will consider.

First, decide what kind of home is desired—parent-centered or child-centered? Second, will decisions be made authoritatively or democratically? Many systems or combinations of systems are acceptable if everyone is satisfied.

Where issues of child discipline are involved, I have found that the most effective form of family government is a benevolent parental dictatorship, i.e. the parents have the final say, but input from the children is invited and always respected, even if not always taken. For instance, children may offer suggestions regarding the type of reinforcing consequences that would please them; more about that later.

GUIDELINES

If you are ready to proceed, here are some guidelines that I recommend:

1. *Consensus:* Parents must agree both on the rules of conduct for everyone (including themselves) and on the consequences for keeping or breaking them. It is not unusual for parents to disagree with each other, but disagreement should be voiced privately. Once agreement is reached, it should be adhered to rigidly.

2. *Conscience:* Are the rules ethical? When do parents have the right or duty to control? Whose best interests are involved? Is power used wisely and fairly? Are the parents being over-controlling or under-controlling?

3. *Contingencies:* Contingencies and consequences can be expressed as "if-then" propositions. If you do that (contingencies), then this will happen (consequences); don't do that, or this will happen. Spell out all the conditions clearly in advance. The more specifically the rules are stated the better. Many families have found that written, signed contracts are effective. They can be posted in a conspicuous place for all to see.

4. *Consequences, Reinforcement and Punishment:* Rewards for positive behaviors are always more effective than punishment for negative behaviors. Why? Because rewards make us happy while punishment make us angry, resentful, resistant, and vengeful. Punishment may stop negative behaviors for the moment; but they will return in the same, different, or often worse forms. Punishment occurs when something we want is taken away or something we don't want is given to us. It is a painful or unpleasant penalty inflicted for wrong-doing. Someone else administers it, and the recipient has no choice but to accept. Punishment is humiliating. Humiliation inevitably diminishes the recipient's self-esteem. If it occurs often enough, the damage can be irreversible.

   Perhaps some further explanations will be helpful here. Technically, rewards are called "reinforcers." When we receive something we want or when something we don't want is removed, behavior is reinforced and, technically, should increase.

The following examples may clarify these concepts.

Positive Reinforcement: "When you have finished your homework, you may watch TV for an hour."

Negative Reinforcement: "You have been good, so you don't have to cut the grass tomorrow."

Punishment: "You didn't do your homework, so no TV for a week.

Negative consequences differ from punishment in that they are fully explained ahead of time, they present choices, and the recipient has a way to end them. For example: "When you have finished your homework, you may watch TV for an hour; no homework, no TV; the choice is up to you." Or, "If you break the rules you will go to time-out. You may come out when you agree to follow the rules. The choice is up to you."

5. *Contiguity:* To increase the likelihood of change, reinforcements should follow behaviors as quickly as possible. Promises of future payment are weak compared to immediate gratification. By the time a future payment comes due, a lot of forgetting (on both sides) can take place.

6. *Choices:* How much does the person being controlled have to say about the plan? Can he or she select his or her own rewards? Participation enhances cooperation.

7. *Consistency:* The most important of all! Once a rule is agreed upon, make no exceptions. Let children know you mean business from the start. They can tell. Remember, *relentless consistency!* There is no place for benevolent exceptions if consistency is to do its job.

Household rules are to be set in stone and put in place as soon as a child is old enough to understand them. They are to become part of the family lore: "That's just the way we do things around here."

Observe the **Never** rules:

- *Never make a rule you cannot enforce.*

- *Never give an order more than once.* If you do, you have already lost authority. Each repetition diminishes your effectiveness.

- *Never argue.* (An argument is a discussion with anger.) If you do, your position has been greatly compromised. Back off until the anger cools.

- *Never shout.* If you do, you have already lost respect and set a poor example. Shouting degrades both you and your children.

- *Never threaten.* Let the contingencies and consequences speak for themselves. There is no need for threats if you follow through.

- *Never bribe.* If you give the reward first, the desired behavior might not occur. I know a father who gave his child a new BMW when he promised to finish his work and graduate from high school. Guess what happened.

- *Never reward or punish a child for academic work.* Let the school handle that. If learning and good grades are not sufficiently rewarding, added incentives may help temporarily but not in the long run. Plato told us long ago, "no forced study abides in the soul," and "bodily exercise, when compulsory, does no harm to the body, but knowledge which is acquired under compulsion obtains no hold on the mind."

- *Never, never, never allow a TV set in a child's or teenager's room.* TV isolates. And no music, video games, or recreational use of a computer during either time-out or study hours. Never! Period! No matter how vehement the argument to the contrary, no one can do two things well simultaneously. Many young people are convinced (and try to convince their parents) that they can study better with music in the background. Physiologically, this is just not so. Our brains are not capable of focusing on more than one thing at a time.

My grandson asked me about the notion that classical music in the background allows for increased brain activity and thus helps in studying. Nice try, Robert. Perhaps classical music does increase brain activity, but that does not mean improved concentration. Classical music, like studies, deserves full concentration. Upon reading my conclusion, our other brilliant grandson, David, took his cousin's side and had the temerity to challenge my theory with facts. His research revealed that classical, ambient music may at times improve concentration. However, he did not identify any studies that found metal, grunge, rock or rap aided concentration.

O.K., maybe I need to back up a little, but I still contend that the listener does a disservice to Mozart by using his incredible artistry as elevator music. And how will the listener's concentration be affected if and when Mozart is not available? I remain convinced that multi-tasking is the mother of mediocrity and still urge handling workloads in series, not in parallel. Do one thing at a time well.

◆ *Never fail to set limits.* Limit TV time, never use TV as a baby sitter; limit recreational computer use, limit video games, limit talking or texting on cell phones.

Never allow cell phone conversations or texting while driving a car. Take away the car if necessary; it's a matter of life or death!

By some estimates, by the end of high school, the average child has seen more than 350,000 TV commercials.

One limit-setting strategy: state and enforce the equivalency rule. For every hour spent on electronic recreation, an equivalent hour must be devoted to constructive reading. No trash! The more time spent reading, the more time may be spent in mindless activity.

Give it a try!

◆ *Never fail to encourage children and adolescents to read.* The sooner the better; read to them as children. Set an example by reading yourself, not just for recreation but also to improve your own knowledge and thinking skills. Also, note that curiosity is the key to concentration. Look for answers in the non-fiction materials you read.

ALLOWANCES

Beware when giving allowances. Allowances can be tricky. Some parents believe they should be given freely so the child will have his or her own spending money. Others believe they should be earned as a way to introduce the child to economics and responsibility.

Some parents believe that chores are the child's responsibility as a member of the household. "That's the way we do things around here. Everyone must pull his own weight." Chores should be expected and not rewarded.

Other parents have found that money provides an excellent means of maintaining household order. I have found that either method may work successfully provided the following rules are observed:

1. Start making the child responsible for household chores as early as he is able to perform them.

2. Set these expectations explicitly and allow a minimum of variation. For example, "Keep your room clean; keep yourself clean; be ready for school on time. No exceptions." Most parents think these duties should be expected and not rewarded. This philosophy is perfectly acceptable as long as obligations are set early and performance strictly enforced.

3. Additional duties may be included and compensated, like taking out the garbage, helping prepare meals, setting the table, doing the dishes, mowing the lawn, taking care of the baby, and helping with housekeeping.

   ♦ **Never pay for chores ahead of time; no advances on allowances, no exceptions!**

These rules will work well provided both parents agree to the terms and conditions, and exceptions are held to a minimum. Monetary payments should not be excessive and should be withheld if the tasks are not performed in a timely fashion. No excuses!

Precision Time-Out

Use precision time-out. Precision time-out is based on the theory that it is more effective to reward positive behaviors than to punish negative behaviors. The idea sounds easy enough, but the execution (perhaps not the best choice of words) requires determination, perseverance and, most important of all, consistency.

Johnny is misbehaving at dinner. He arrives late, declares he hates the food, and throws a bread roll at his kid sister. The punishing parents respond, "You have been a bad boy. You are going to bed without supper. No TV for a week!" The non-punishing parents protest, "John please stop that; you know how it upsets us."

> SOME PARENTS BELIEVE THAT NOT ALLOWING A CHILD TO COMPLETE A MEAL IS CRUEL AND UNUSUAL PUNISHMENT. IT IS CERTAINLY NOT UNUSUAL, AND CRUELTY SEEMS AN OVERSTATEMENT. THE CHILD WON'T STARVE ...

The practice of precision time-out goes something like this: "Johnny, this kind of behavior is not acceptable in our home. You will either stop what you have been doing or go to time- out. The choice is up to you. You may come out when you can behave responsibly." Period! No argument, no exceptions and no anger! Parental anger gives youngsters too many feelings of power that they are not ready to handle. And let's not forget that the best place for time-out is a room with nothing available except useful reading or studying material.

Precision time-out works best within certain guidelines.

If precision time-out is to be used successfully as a substitute for punishment for unacceptable behavior, it is essential that rules of conduct be clearly understood from the beginning and that all consequences for rule-breaking are also clearly understood by everyone.

Here is one more very important concept. Technically, it is called "intermittent reinforcement." It means that as long as hope (or chance) is present, people will develop habits that are nearly impossible to break. Take gambling. People know ahead of time that the odds are highly stacked against them. Nevertheless, they keep on playing so long as there is even a faint glimmer of hope. If there is no hope, there will be no more playing.

How does this notion apply to parenting? As long as children think the parents may change the rules even once, they will keep on trying to have their way. So, never vary. Once a rule is set, let them know it will not be changed. They have to know you mean business! Take curfew. If it is set at 10:30 p.m., that means 10:30 p.m., not 10:31 p.m. If the rule is broken, let the agreed upon consequences take over. No arguing, no excuses, no exceptions! For example, "The new curfew will be at 10:00 p.m. When you come in by 10:00 p.m. for four consecutive times, it can go back to 10:30 p.m. It's up to you."

Remember, relentless consistency.

The earlier these principles are applied the better. Early crying outbursts and temper tantrums can be eradicated by applying these suggestions as soon as these unpleasant behaviors occur. The longer parents procrastinate and tolerate the behavior, the more difficult it becomes to apply the principles. Here's another example:

Sallie cries at the supper table and won't eat her food. Mom states, "Sallie, your crying and not eating are not O.K.; either stop crying and start eating, or you may be excused and go to time-out. The choice is up to you. When you stop crying you may return and join us. That too is up to you." Notice, there is no arguing, no scolding, no threats, no yelling, no parental anger and, perhaps, no dinner.

To extinguish an unacceptable behavior, rather than punishing it, reinforce a competing acceptable behavior. For example, don't punish shouting, praise quiet; or don't punish not eating; just remove the food, wait for hunger to set in (no snacks), and then praise the inevitable eating when it occurs.

Some parents believe that not allowing a child to complete a meal is cruel and unusual punishment. It is certainly not unusual, and cruelty seems an overstatement. The child won't starve, and the beneficial effects of this stern but fair action can be enormous and long lasting. It has worked in our family.

Remember, no one is ready to assume the responsibility of freedom until he or she has learned to accept the discipline of limitations.

9
TEACHING TEENS

This essay is dedicated to John, Allie, Meredith, Michael, Lindsey, and Laura—all special Sunday school students. My thanks and love for helping teach me how to teach you.

I have been working with teenagers in one capacity or another since I was fourteen: camp counselor, dorm counselor, Sunday school teacher, classroom teacher, parent, grandparent, and psychotherapist. I hope these young people learned something from me; I know I have learned a great deal from them. Here are some ideas that I hope will be helpful to teachers:

WHEN I TALK WITH YOUNG PEOPLE ABOUT SEX, I DISCOVER TWO REMARKABLE FACTS. FIRST, THEY ALREADY KNOW MORE THAN I MAY GUESS AND, SECOND, THEY DON'T KNOW NEARLY AS MUCH AS THEY SHOULD.

- Show you care about your students; have their best interests at heart. They can spot a phony in no time.

- Be scrupulously honest, especially about yourself.

- Listen to your students more than you talk to them.

- Find out where *they* are with a subject before you tell them where *you* are.

- Ask lots of questions.

- Talk *with* them, not *to* them.

- Be interested in and respectful of their ideas and beliefs.

- Don't lecture; don't preach.

- Constantly ask for feedback; find out what they are hearing.

- Stay aware of their feelings and respond accordingly.

- Don't try to tell them too much at once; settle for a few points well understood rather than a litany to which they are indifferent.

- Keep the agenda flexible so you can adjust your message as you hear their reactions.

- Find out what they want to discuss; it may not be what you want to present.

- Never, never, never talk down to them.

- Display a gentle sense of humor; it is essential, sets them at ease, and keeps you from taking yourself too seriously.

- Know the topic under discussion thoroughly so you can talk to them, not read to them, except perhaps a brief quotation or two. Spontaneous offerings are much more effective than rehearsed presentations.

Along that line, and in my role as a teacher, here are the subjects that I have found to be of the most interest to the teenagers whom I have had the pleasure of knowing well and the privilege of teaching:

- Themselves
- Sex
- Addictions
- Emotions, Moods and Mental Health
- Education, Careers, Money
- Religion and Philosophy

THEMSELVES

Teenagers, like most of us, are preoccupied with themselves. I tell them that there is nothing wrong with that. It is perfectly normal as long as they don't get carried away with it.

As a matter of fact, being totally unselfish is very difficult.

I usually ask them what the "self" is. How do you define it? There are many definitions, but my favorite is to explain that our brain has at least three levels: conscious, unconscious (or subconscious), and under-conscious, all of which are part of ourselves. We could talk about ego, id, and super-ego but they, and I, tend to get lost in all that psychological jargon.

I explain that our first brain level is the "conscious," the part of ourselves that is aware, and where we think and imagine and fantasize. The second level, the "unconscious" (or "subconscious"), is where our personal memories are stored. They can be reached through dreams, contemplation, prayer, and bursts of sudden insight ("aha!" moments).

The third and most complex level, which I call the "under- conscious," is, I believe, where C.G. Jung's (1964) "collective unconscious" resides. The under-conscious harbors the memories, insights, and wisdom common to all humankind. The term used by the French philosopher René Descartes was "eternal verities." I have found that there is also a second component, an "ancestral unconscious," where our "genie" resides.

Our ancestral unconscious is the home of attributes unique to each individual. This repository also houses our genie, a spiritual presence capable of transporting these qualities into conscious awareness. The genie is the "voice" of our personal inherent characteristics. How does it work?

Well, an example from my own experience goes like this:

I can't compose a suitable melody for a song I am writing. I have the words, but the melody just isn't there. So, I give up struggling, try to clear my mind, and wait. Maybe it comes, maybe not. If not, I wait a little longer. Often I can feel the presence of my grandfather, a fine old German musician and composer, brought to me compliments of my genie. Then I take a shower (my wife appreciates that) and start singing the words at the top of my voice. What happens? Sometimes nothing, but more often than not the melody comes, loud and clear. I jump out of the shower, dripping wet, to capture it on my recorder before it vanishes. Sound crazy? I love it!

Some of us, I explain to teens, think we don't have any talent. Maybe we just haven't found it yet or haven't looked deeply enough. Is God fair? Why should some people burst with talents while others don't seem to have been blessed with any?

I believe the answer lies in the ancestral unconscious. Everyone has an abundance of talents. Maybe those talents are buried deeper than those that show up early in others, or maybe negative feelings such as anger, depression, or fear are blocking them. I urge teens to start listening and looking and trying; they may be amazed at what they find. The Greek word for "spirit" is "genius," like a genie. The question here is not, "Are you a genius?" but rather, "Have you found your genie?" To those who have found their genie, I say, "Use him." I encourage those who have not to look deeper within. It's there, a special skill, talent, or gift passed on as a hidden heritage from our ancestors. Perhaps it is poetry, composing, sculpting, painting, dancing, gardening, sewing, compassionate caretaking, teaching, or a combination unique to the individual. I promise: the hidden creativity is there.

Now, listening without thinking is not an easy art to perfect. One must teach oneself to hear that "still small voice of calm" (1 Kings). Listen for the sacred presence in silence. Perhaps it is the Holy Spirit; perhaps it is the genie. Perhaps they are the same.

So I tell teens, if they have a problem, a decision to be reached or an unfinished creation—wait. Sleep on it, and the inspiration will come. Take in all the advice, suggestions, and information available. The final decision rests with the individual, and it will be found at that third level of consciousness.

The answers lie within. Be patient, settle down, and listen to the genie.

Many therapists, including me, have found that personal wholeness is best achieved when all three levels of consciousness are integrated. With integration, the conscious becomes aware of and feels the power and energy of the unconscious, and the under-conscious reveals the "fruits of the spirit" so the conscious can put them to use. I suggest that each individual should first "uncork the genie" and let the genie help "liberate creativity" that can lead to happiness. For more on this, refer to Chapter 4, "The Ancestral Unconscious: Uncorking Your Genie."

Sex

When I talk with young people about sex, I discover two remarkable facts. First, they already know more than I may guess and, second, they don't know nearly as much as they should. I ask them where they learned what they know. It is seldom from their parents. Why not? The answer is that both they and their parents are often too embarrassed to discuss such delicate matters candidly with one another.

So where do they go? To peers, of course; but peers don't know enough either, and what they do know is often incorrect nonsense. To the Internet? Dreadful! To TV? Deplorable! To the family doctor? Not often enough, and then they usually discuss the physical, not the emotional side of sexuality. Ministers too are often helpful but are seldom sought. And they deal mostly with the moral aspects. Many schools conduct sex education classes, but they are often highly controversial and, therefore, get watered down to lectures with charts, diagrams, and discussions of anatomical rather than emotional factors and consequences.

As both a psychologist and Sunday-school teacher I feel that I have been in a unique position to help. I must acknowledge that some parents and ministers do not agree that Sunday school or church is an acceptable place to discuss sexual issues. I am sorry about that, because I cannot think of a better place. So here are my thoughts:

Birth Control

This is a tough one. Some religions oppose contraception altogether, teaching that sex is intended only for procreation. I'm afraid this notion is rather unrealistic. Some churches and parents urge abstinence for their youngsters, a beautiful idea that works well in some cases. But in today's world, where recreational sex is shown everywhere, where being "hot" means being sexy and popular, virginity is looked on as un-cool and hopelessly old-fashioned.

> THE "MORNING AFTER" PILL IS A STEP IN THE RIGHT DIRECTION. TO LABEL IT A FORM OF ABORTION, ONCE AGAIN RAISING THE ISSUE OF GUILT, IS ONE MORE ATTEMPT TO AVOID FACING THE ISSUE OF UNWANTED PREGNANCIES AND OVER-POPULATION.

Abstinence is also fraught with danger. One slip, one moment where temptation, drugs, alcohol or the phrase, "you will if you love me" are present can upend lives for many people—the unwanted child, the teen-aged parents and their families.

According to current research, while hundreds of thousands of dollars have been spent on abstinence-only programs, they simply don't work! Actually, wherever the programs have been tried, pregnancy rates increased. So my question is this: What is a more realistic sex education program?

My suggestion for the essentials of such a program would include the following:

1. Contraception
2. Spiritual sexuality
3. Abortion versus the unwanted child – "pro-qual" (pro quality of life)
4. Dress code
5. Sobriety

Note: For girls, I say that if a boy tries to persuade you to have sex and you don't want to, then you don't want him. And to boys, I point out that if a girl gives sex away, you don't want her.

Contraception: In my personal and professional opinion, contraception is a must. Condoms may protect against disease and pregnancy, but they present many drawbacks. They are expensive, not always available when needed, messy, are sometimes unreliable, curtail romantic spontaneity, and prevent the physical intimacy that goes with natural intercourse. Until something better is developed, however, as my friend and colleague, Vickie Harkins, told me, "using condoms is no longer a choice; it is a must."

Contraceptive pills and condoms, while not yet perfect, should be made available at the lowest possible cost to anyone who might even remotely be a candidate for sexual activity, especially for anyone who drinks or uses drugs. Perhaps, as some argue, this use of contraception may increase the chances of promiscuity; but, this possibility is far overshadowed by the potential tragedy of unwanted pregnancy.

The "morning after" pill is a step in the right direction. To label it a form of abortion, once again raising the issue of guilt, is one more attempt to avoid facing the issue of unwanted pregnancies and over-population.

What more can be done? We should urge our governments to concentrate on contraceptive research. We need a pill or a vaccine for both men and women that will prevent both conception and sexually transmitted diseases and that can be distributed worldwide either at no cost or at prices that everyone can afford.

Certainly this is a huge order, but can anyone think of a better way to spend our money? Overpopulation is, or should be, ranked as the world's greatest problem. Our environment becomes more and more polluted as increasing masses of people use up resources, and reduce the quality of life for the whole world.

Spiritual Sexuality: Men and women are conditioned to react emotionally in different ways. Fair or not, a man with many conquests is too often regarded (usually with admiration and envy) as a "player." A promiscuous woman on the other hand is too often regarded derogatively as a "slut." Is that unjust? Of course, and the consequences run even deeper than that.

For many men, in my experience at least, the thrill of the hunt, the chase and the "kill" requires degrees of ever-changing variety in frantic attempts to satisfy a lust that excludes love. For many women, often it appears to be the thrill of seduction, the power of entrapment, the continued affirmation of their desirability, or the belief that this is the only way to keep a man.

None of these charades endures, requiring the games to start all over again until the players are burned out. Why? Because lust is always a form of masturbation, using the partner as a means of satisfying one's own needs with no concern for the relationship or the consequences. Sooner or later satiety sets in. The participants inevitably become jaded, bored, callous, cynical, and unable to experience the wonders of spiritual sexuality.

There are critical distinctions between "being in lust," "being in love," and "being infused." "In lust" translates to unrestrained sexual desire that is totally self-serving. On the other hand, "In love" translates to mutually shared, physical attraction. The problem with trying to have a permanent partnership based on "being in love" is that when the fizz fizzles, as is inevitable, the partners may begin to see each other in an entirely new and not always enduring light.

"Being infused" is a joining of two souls that complete one another. This union is the prerequisite for achieving "spiritual sexuality."

Spiritual sexuality involves putting the welfare of your partner above your own. It means seeking and discovering the person behind the sexual facade, so that being together becomes enjoyable in itself and is only enriched by mutually satisfying, sexual experiences that value caring above carnality.

Spiritual sexuality requires work and takes time, perhaps a lifetime. It requires an understanding and appreciation of the personality of the partner and an unselfishness that keeps the romance alive. It means a joining of spirits. It can provide lasting satisfactions and joys such as trust, loyalty and integrity that remain long after the orgasms. I believe it to be universally true that lustful intercourse cannot touch the ecstasy of intercourse where both bodies and spirits unite.

Abortion: Decisions about abortion are hard on everyone, especially the woman. I wish legislators and judges (mostly men) would get beyond arguing about "life and choice" and about making abortion a crime.

The issue would be better framed as discussion about the lesser of two evils: destroying a fetus or adding another unwanted life to an already over-populated planet.

I believe that after medical, psychological and legal consultations with parents, the final decision should be left to the expectant parents, if they are mentally and emotionally competent. The decision should be reached and implemented as early as possible. If she chooses to terminate the pregnancy, the woman should be praised for her courage in not bringing another unwanted life into this over-populated world rather than being made to feel guilty about her decision.

The so-called "morning-after" pill, controversial as it may be, presents an excellent alternative until better contraceptive techniques are perfected. That pill should be available to anyone who has had sexual intercourse and who does not want to become pregnant. In any case, the pregnant woman should be treated with compassion and understanding and never made to feel guilty; and the man must always accept mutual responsibility.

One other point to stress: there is an attitude that casual sex (of course, there is no such thing) without contraception may be indulged in because the woman "can always get an abortion." What is often misunderstood is that an abortion is always a tragic event. While, along with adoption, it is an alternative to be preferred over creating an unwanted child, the emotional scars are always long-standing. Most women recover in time, but the feelings experienced may never be entirely erased. Let's add a third component to the debate between pro-life and pro-choice: quality of life. Let's consider "pro-qual."

I have read recently that some public schools have forbidden hugging in the hallways or perhaps anywhere on school property. What a shame! I love hugging. In sixty years of working with young people, only once have I been criticized for hugging a student. I have no intention of stopping this practice, but now I ask ahead of time if it's okay. For heaven's sake! Have you ever met anyone beyond the age of puberty who didn't instantly know the difference between a sexual hug and an affectionate one? And so many of us need affection desperately!

Dress Code: Now, this is a really tough one! Look at the examples set by advertising, music videos, movies and TV, teen stars and other "personalities." The key image is "being hot."

In my experience, what men find to be sexually attractive in women are curves, softness, and smoothness. I am less sure about what women find sexy in men, but I suppose it is muscle definition, strength and hardness. Opposites attract, and Freud did know a thing or two about that. If young women want to be provocative, they will wear high heels and tight pants or short skirts so that both their tops and bottoms protrude alluringly. To top all that off, so to speak, they will add low-cut blouses and push-up bras to complete this seductive display. Some young men also wear sleeveless shirts, open down the front, and tight pants. Dressing to reveal as much of their bodies as possible, even if just following fashion trends, can lead to sexually explosive situations long before the individual is emotionally prepared to handle them.

If parents and school authorities want to cut back teen promiscuity, I suggest they insist on more modest dress codes and not allow their children to leave home dressed in any way that might be considered revealing or provocative. Also, they might want to take a look at their own styles of dressing.

Addictions: Caffeine, nicotine, over-eating, gambling, drugs, other external stimulants, and alcohol can be addictive. They are all harmful and dangerous; and, once they enter our bodies and minds, form habits that are extremely difficult to break. So why do people use them? Are we self-destructive? Do we not want to hear the truth? Do we put a higher value on our pleasures than on our health, or do we try things because they are forbidden fruits, like the apples in Eden?

- *Caffeine:* Caffeine is probably the least harmful of these addictive substances. It does help many people wake up and face a new day. It can also make us hyper, nervous, and disturb our sleep. In the long run, it contributes to poor health. Is it worth it? My suggestion: stay away from excessive amounts of coffee and potent caffeine drinks.

- *Nicotine:* Former U.S. Surgeon General C. Everett Koop told us years ago that smoking is more addictive and a harder habit to conquer than heroin! With all we know today, why anyone ever starts is beyond me. How stupid can we be?

  Do kids think smoking is cool and looks grown up? It isn't, and it doesn't. It just looks foolish. Is it rebellion against authority? If so, there are certainly less self-destructive ways to rebel.

  I smoked a pipe and little cigars for forty years and loved every puff. I quit, cold turkey, more than twenty years ago because my mother asked me to and because I was getting more and more colds and coughs. I don't miss the little cigars, but I still yearn for a pipe full of aromatic tobacco in the evenings on my screened porch.

- *Over-Eating:* Most of us do not think of over-eating as an addiction, but it is increasingly recognized as a health issue. If over-eating begins early, it can cause a lifetime of problems. Obesity is unattractive, harmful to health and long life. Added weight can be terribly hard to lose.

  The Germans have a saying, "Das appetit kommt mit dem essen" (Appetite comes with eating). The more we eat, in other words, the more we want to eat. Conversely, if we stop eating certain foods, we can learn to do without them. I know; I was a cookie monster. After a period of forcing myself not to enjoy them regularly, I lost my craving. Although one cookie every now and then is still delightful, that one cookie now tastes better than a whole handful used to. Try it.

There are a lot of well-advertised diets out there but the one that works best for me is simply "eat less; exercise more."

- ◆ *Gambling:* Gambling is perhaps the most subtle, seductive, and ruinous (other than drugs) of the addictions. It sneaks up on its victims and leaves broken lives, broken families, and broken fortunes in its wake.

  It has become even more dangerous since it was legalized in so many places. Its subtle and crafty sponsors use good works such as support of education, seductively, to justify its use. They never mention its dreadful effects, especially on those poor folks who can least afford it.

  Gambling forms habits that are almost impossible to break, because it is based on the sound learning theory of "intermittent reinforcement." That theory holds that as long as chance or hope is present, human beings will keep on trying, even though the odds are almost insurmountable. In gambling, excitement adds to the momentary pleasure.

  The old adage of "never gamble more than you can afford to lose" is sound as far as it goes, but more often than not, it isn't strong enough to overcome the promise (usually false) of big pay-offs. The best advice (so often not taken) is "don't start."

- ◆ *Drugs:* The best advice I know about starting or experimenting with drugs is don't do it. Period! Unfortunately, peer pressure is so enormous that many young people can't withstand the urge to go along with the crowd. Drug use seems to be an effective way to wage rebellion against parents and society. *But, but, but,* even more so than with alcohol, I have never known anyone, young or old, whose life was improved through the use of illicit drugs. So many lives have been, or are still being, ruined beyond repair by drugs. Even if someone can kick the habit, the residual effects will last a lifetime. No one is ever the same after using drugs even for a short time.

  Does this apply to marijuana? Oh, yes! There are many arguments about the pleasurable and harmless effects of marijuana. They simply are not true! The use of marijuana too often leads to the use of other even more harmful drugs. Marijuana is highly addictive, debilitating, enervating, and brain damaging. It saps motivation and ambition and the desire to learn. In its way, it is a form of nonviolent rebellion—rebelling by doing nothing. In the end the main damage is done to the mind of the user. And, once again, the rebellious user is merely swapping one kind of dependence for another. How pathetic!

How do we persuade youngsters not to start? Peer pressure is the best influence; example can be effective, showing it to be "un-cool." We should never, ever consider legalizing the sale of marijuana. Perhaps its use in terminal cases of otherwise "unrelievable" pain can be justified if under the supervision of a physician, but that's all.

As for other, even more damaging non-prescription and so-called "recreational" drugs, just watch a few episodes of entertainment news programs on TV. You will see an endless array of movie and TV personalities, rock stars, and athletes whose lives, families, careers and minds will never be the same. When will we learn? God's greatest gift to the human race is a clear brain. It is so important to take care of that marvelous and irreplaceable organ.

Hallucinogens are even more dreadful. Many years ago, I worked for a year with a teen-aged, female in-patient at Central State Hospital in Milledgeville, Georgia. She had used LSD and suffered from horrifying flashbacks and long, stupefying blackouts. *She never improved.* In spite of medications and extensive psychotherapy, she never improved. I am told that hallucinogens bring weird and colorful pictures to the brain. Even if true, hallucinogens can also destroy forever the natural ability to imagine.

♦ *External stimulants:* Video games, social media, and other external stimulants can be addictive, too. Caffeine, food, nicotine, alcohol and drugs are all internal addictive substances that allegedly make us "feel better," while lowering brain cell production. External stimulants can also engender deleterious effects in our brains. Parents and educators should take a hard look at television, computer games, smart phones, and the endless flow of electronic gadgetry. How many hours a day are wastefully consumed by activities that contribute absolutely nothing positive to the intellectual reasoning left hemisphere of the brain? Current research informs us that average Internet use is approximately 18 hours a week; that's almost three hours a day.

Notice that all of these activities provide external stimulation, leaving little or no time for the internal applications of imagination, calculation, contemplation, reasoning and creativity. No wonder we are raising automatons with very short attention spans who become restless and bored if there is "nothing to do" and regard serious reading or thinking as old-fashioned, dull and un-cool.

You will hear vigorous arguments from young people that computer games, video games, and other gadgetry, improve eye-hand coordination and reaction skills, but that is all right-brain stuff and doesn't affect the left hemisphere skills of critical thinking, problem-solving, inventive thinking, intellectual memory and math and reading skills. If young people require games to hold their attention, tell them to go retro and try "sim" computer games, which force players to build and govern fictional societies. Or young people can tackle old-fashioned crossword puzzles, which exercise the left side of the brain. If youth need to develop greater proficiency in word games, they should try the soon-to-be-released computer game called GOcabulary® Plus. It is an efficient and enjoyable way to improve vocabulary and reading skills (check gocabulary.com). It also forces players to use both the left and right hemispheres of their brains.

One more thought along this line. Are there negative consequences to the proliferating use of computers, smart phones, and various other gadgets? Well, the more we use computers to solve complex problems, the less we need to use our minds. Does overuse of these devices retard our ability to conceptualize critically or creatively? Does storing information electronically inhibit our mental retrieval skills? And, finally, does using email and text messaging sacrifice eloquence for brevity, profound expression for speed, and intimacy for popularity? Are we in danger of rearing a new generation of cyborgs?

◆   *Alcohol:* Alcohol is a tough subject to talk about with young people, primarily because so many adults use it to some degree or other. The only way to be effective with teenagers is to share your own views and experience after they have told you where they stand. They live with tremendous peer pressure, but I urge them to search within themselves and then make, and take responsibility for, their own decisions.

Here are the views that I hold. First, I have never known anyone—friend, acquaintance, or patient—who was any better off for having used alcohol in any form. I have known a lot of people whose lives have been diminished, turned upside down, or ruined by alcohol.

While there may be an alcoholic personality, over many years of working with alcoholics I have come to the conclusion that anyone who drinks regularly over an extended period of time can, and probably will, become an alcoholic.

I have consumed spirits, wine and beer over the years, and they can all leave damaging effects. I have been drunk a few times and then promised myself "never again." Now I stick to it. I don't like what drinking does to my mind, my conduct or my relationships with others; and I don't enjoy being out of control or feeling my brain turn numb.

If a person has to drink to have a good time, it won't take long before he or she can't have a good time without drinking—hazardous territory because alcohol is incredibly habit forming.

Remember, there is no such thing as a free drink.

My wife and I enjoy an occasional glass of wine with dinner on weekends or special occasions. The problem, for me at least, is that if I drink more than one glass of wine in the evening, it slows down my mind so that all I am fit for is TV watching or vapid novel reading. Nothing instructive or constructive follows, just a waste of time! So, I usually prefer not to drink alcohol at all.

At cocktail parties, I observe the "one wine only" rule. I find that I have a much better time than I used to, and I am always reminded that drinking alters the mind.

I used to ask my students to try an experiment. I called it the "joys of not drinking." Go to a party where drinking and getting drunk is expected, but don't participate. Drink a cola and observe objectively what is going on around you. Are the party-goers having fun, or is the alcohol doing it for them? If binge drinking is going on, can you recognize how devastatingly, pathetically and stupidly destructive this practice is?

Remember, I told my students, if you have to drink in order to enjoy yourself, it will not take long to get to the point where you can't enjoy yourself without drinking.

I warn them that, unchecked, they risk developing a lifetime dependence on alcohol. Then I ask if that prospect is appealing.

So, if teenagers can enjoy themselves without dependence on alcohol, they should take pride in that independence, and exert a good and healthy influence on family and friends. And if teenagers turn to alcohol as an act of rebellion against parental dependence, the teens must ask themselves if they are just trading one form of dependence for another, much more destructive one.

THE MODERATION GENERATION©

How do we contemplative and concerned adults begin to turn around this mindless march toward mediocrity?

Ever since the end of Prohibition, there have been numerous, anti-alcohol campaigns directed toward teenagers. These have been largely unsuccessful, I believe, because alcohol consumption among adults is pervasive in today's culture.

Millions more dollars have been poured down the drains of anti-drunk-driving campaigns, because teenagers feel impervious and wrap themselves in the armor of "that won't happen to me." Parents could begin by checking their own drinking behavior. How about trying "if you won't, I won't." That would test parental sincerity. Peer pressures are enormous. The urge to fit in is almost irresistible and being "bad" is so much more fun that being "good."

So, I believe a new approach is necessary. What would happen if a few inventive parents helped create an innovative social club called *Moderation Generation©*? Membership could include adults and adolescents. Moreover, it could be organized along the same lines as other international fraternities or sororities with chapters, small dues to cover expenses, and a monthly publication that could be scientifically informative. The publication also could contain current research findings, personal success stories and humorous anecdotes. Above all, it could share helpful suggestions for curbing alcohol and drug abuse. Members could wear *Moderation Generation©* pins and perhaps hold regular meetings and annual conferences.

Here are some examples of the types of materials that might be included in all *Moderation Generation©* publications:

HUMOR PAGE
Wisdom

Examples:

- *Drinking liquefies thinking!*

- *Boozers are losers!*

- *"It doesn't require a miracle to turn wine into water."*

Appeals to vanity

Examples:

♦ A recent study revealed that smoking marijuana causes early wrinkles, dry skin and acne in brunettes. Also, "blondes who drink red wine may need make-up to hide red noses."

♦ Prizes could be awarded for slogans, poems or cartoons that are included in the publication.

RESEARCH

Alcohol consumption has been shown to retard the generation of new brain cells. Thousands of new cells are generated in the adult brain every day, particularly in the hippocampus. Difficult learning, which involves concentration and critical thinking, helps keep these neurons alive.

Other research has shown that drinkers had about 10 percent smaller hippocampi—the location in the brain that handles memory and learning. Researchers call such a reduction significant and possibly irreversible! Neuroscientists have concluded that alcohol use during the adolescent years is associated with damage to memory and learning capabilities as well as to the decision-making and reasoning areas in the brain.

These researchers also have concluded that alcohol takes a greater toll on the brain development of those under twenty-one than on any other age group. Findings indicate that adults would have to consume twice as many drinks to suffer the same damage as adolescents and that even occasional heavy drinking injures young brains.

EMOTIONS, MOODS AND MENTAL HEALTH

The three, main, negative emotions affecting teenagers, and the rest of us, are anger, anxiety and depression. I discussed anger at some depth in Chapters 2, 3 and 4, so I will only summarize the major points here.

ANGER

The most common type of anger presents a choice. If we are frustrated, hurt, insulted, or diminished, we can choose reactions other than angry ones. Try humor, compassion, understanding, rationalizing, or indifference. Clinging to anger also represents a choice. Whether we do so or not usually depends upon how we feel about ourselves. The better we feel, the less need we have to choose to stay angry, usually blaming something on someone else.

Remember: no one can "make you angry" unless you choose to allow it.

ANXIETY

Anxieties or fears seem to lie right beneath our angry emotions. They are often not acknowledged or understood. They may be labeled "nerves." Left unattended, anxiety or fear can be extremely difficult to live with. Where do these problems come from? Genes, for a start: worrying parents breed worried children; society is another source. We live in such frightening times that existential anxiety has become a way of life for many of us.

Both parents and children live under a mountain of pressure. Do well in high school so you can get into college and have a good career. Produce at your job; make a lot of money; put in sixty-hour or more work weeks, yet still take time for the family; take care of others before yourself; the list goes on. We don't get enough time for sleep and don't take time to relax. Are there solutions? I have found it helpful to suggest that people at almost any age need to stop! Stop right where they are and think, think about values: What is important to them? Where do they want to go? What kind of people do they want to be or become? At the end of their lives when they look back, what do they want to see? Finally and most important, what will make them feel good about themselves?

These kinds of reflections can relieve a great deal of anxiety. As with anger, the answers are not "out there." They lie within.

DEPRESSION

Depression is a far more serious emotional state than either anger or anxiety, because all too often it leads to suicide. Sadness generally has an external cause such as a loss or failure. It usually passes or at least lessens with time. Depression is more complex. It usually contains components of both anger and fear and can be an inherited condition.

Modern medicines have made giant steps in the treatment of genetic or physiological depressions. Restoring chemical balances can work wonders, especially in conjunction with psychotherapy.

Often, naive if well-intentioned parents, friends, or even professionals offer such useless advice as "snap out of it" or "just pull yourself together and stop feeling sorry for yourself." If they haven't been there, they cannot understand. A depressed mood, like any other painful emotion, turns us entirely in upon ourselves. We can think or care about nothing else. I have found that cognitive therapy or "positive thinking" is not particularly effective in cases of severe depression; it is impossible to think well of ourselves when severely depressed.

To deal with depression, I have used a three-fold path toward restoring health both for myself and others: appropriate medications; insightful, supportive, non-judgmental psychotherapies, preferably with a therapist who has been there; and a lot of love and understanding.

OCD AND OCP

Another disturbing mental health problem is Obsessive Compulsive Disorder (OCD). Symptoms can range from a minor irritation, like double-checking to make sure the lights are off, to major disturbances such as thought fixations and never-ending rituals. Medications and cognitive-behavioral therapies can help relieve this disorder.

Obsessive Compulsive Personality (OCP) is a more benign condition. A person with OCP may be preoccupied with details, rules, lists and the necessity to maintain order. Also, such personalities may make themselves and others uncomfortable if everything is not perfect.

People with OCP have achieved many great accomplishments in this world. If individuals have this type of personality, they can use it to their advantage by changing the focus of that energy stream from constant worrying to creative productivity. They can learn to write, paint, compose, sculpt, garden, weave, study, learn, build, or start a new project. The possibilities are many. That is how an OCP can be transformed into an OCCP (Obsessive Compulsive Creative Personality).

HAPPINESS

This may be a good place to talk about happiness. I have spent some time talking with happy people. Here are some of their secrets.

First, maintain good health. It is hard to be happy when you feel miserable physically.

Second, happiness comes, not surprisingly, from two places, internal and external. Happy people have found that internal happiness comes from feeling good about themselves, possessing self-confidence, and from the ability to find *"large pleasures in small treasures."*

Third, they achieve external happiness through the simple but sometimes difficult process of "giving back," doing something for others. A wealthy man I know practices personal giving back. Every time he buys some luxury item for himself, he gives something of equal value or an equivalent amount of money to a needy person or charitable cause. It makes him feel happy and relieves his guilt. More than money, happy people usually give something of themselves—a personal touch. That could be something as simple as focusing on who a person is and not on what he or she does to earn a living. A graduate student of mine told me years ago that the key to happiness is "Don't take it personally." I would add "Make the best of it and move on."

The Egyptian requirements for entrance into heaven were based on the responses to the following questions:

- Has your life brought you joy?

- Has your life brought joy to others?

Of course, joy is even better than happiness.

THOUGHTS VS. FEELINGS

I worked recently with an eighteen-year-old, high school senior who did not grasp the difference between thoughts and feelings. I suspect that he is not alone. Following are some thoughts about thoughts, and thoughts about feelings.

Thoughts are concepts or ideas. They are expressed through words and sentences. Feelings are emotions that may be described by words but are experienced as tangible presences in the body. Feelings are often difficult to describe. When we ask people how they feel, often they reply by telling us what they think. Let's try to clarify.

The primary feelings are mad, sad, glad and afraid. They have remained throughout the evolutionary survival processes to support fighting, compassion, procreation and flight. The secondary emotions are more complex and more difficult to define since they contain elements of the primary feelings.

Secondary emotions would include the following:

- Power: strength, invincibility

- Weakness: helplessness, impotence, vulnerability

- Shame: guilt, humiliation

- Embarrassment: awkward moments, "oops" experiences

Moods are extended feelings:

- Depression: extended sadness

- Joy: extended happiness

- Anxiety: extended fear

- Hatred: extended anger

Which are more influential on our behavior? Cognitive therapists will insist that thoughts can control feelings. Certainly, this is true to some extent; but

I have found that, more often, the opposite proves true. There is a difference between an emotion and a feeling. An emotion is a sensation experienced in the body. A feeling is the mental interpretation of that emotion.

EDUCATION, CAREERS AND MONEY

The purpose of a good education can be summed up in two words, "employment and enjoyment." In 1947, Dean James Leyburn at Washington and Lee University told me that "the purpose of a liberal arts education is to teach us how to spend our leisure time." Abraham Maslow (1954) spoke of need hierarchies by which he meant it was necessary to satisfy the more basic needs such as nourishment, shelter, and clothing before pursuing the higher goals of art, music, or literature.

When young people are trying to decide what to do with their lives, I suggest to them that they think about goals. What is important to them? What will give them satisfaction and help them feel good about themselves? What will give their lives purpose? Asking (and answering) such questions is especially important for students entering high school. They risk wasting four years in high school, graduating with no idea about what they want to study in college and thereby squandering another four precious years of their young lives, to say nothing of the expenses involved.

Paying for young people to attend college with no idea of what they want to do with their lives is wasteful for everyone: the young person, the parents and the college. If they need to "find themselves," college is not the place to do it. Let them find a job, grow up, get some experience, go into community service, take an apprenticeship, and then consider what kind of education will be most useful. Such a student heads to college with purpose, determination and enthusiasm.

When I went to Georgia Tech in the 1940s, the best students were the ones in the work-study programs. They attended classes for one or two semesters then worked for a company in their field for the next semester. They earned tuition money, got invaluable experience and had a job waiting for them upon graduation. Earning the degree took five years with no summer vacations, but they had the pride of paying their own way, didn't use college just as a place to party, really knew their stuff, and were ahead in their careers.

If a student decides to go to college, he or she must learn how to study. Here are some tips: learn to read, read, read! And learn how to concentrate on that reading.

Remember, multi-tasking is the mother of mediocrity.

Our minds cannot concentrate on more than one thing at a time. No music, phone, or TV while studying! No browsing, no video games until after study time! Never, no way, never!

When reading, I have found it helpful to underline important passages, flagging them for later study. This method is far preferable to reading the same things over and over. Another useful technique while reading complex material is to think of a question and then see if you can find the answer as you proceed. Looking for answers is why mysteries and page-turners are so fascinating and capture the reader's attention. You can apply the same techniques to your non-fiction work and find that it can be just as enjoyable.

Curiosity intensifies both concentration and retention, so *stay curious* and keep your dictionary handy. Never skip over a word you can't define, or you won't achieve understanding. This practice can lead you directly to the *joy of learning*—a treasure that can last a lifetime.

Finally, as an aside to multi-tasking, take a pledge not to drive while on a cell phone talking, texting, or checking email. It is a danger to yourself and others as you must take one hand off the wheel and your mind off careful driving.

Remember, college is a privilege, not a pastime!

Lucky—or wise—students have a solid idea of what they want to be well ahead of time: doctors, lawyers, teachers, politicians, engineers, caregivers, etc. Others seek knowledge either for its own sake or because of a consuming curiosity for biology, history, science, or literature. They know where they want to go and who or what they want to be. They don't need much help in getting there.

These fortunate young souls pursue their educational goals with a determination that doesn't leave much time for clouding their minds with alcohol or drugs. Most youngsters, sadly, are not in these scholarly categories and need help making major educational decisions. Here are some things to consider:

- Do you want your life to be self-centered or other-centered?
- Is your goal to get rich or to make a comfortable living?
- Will you take a job you don't enjoy but which pays well over one you love that pays less?
- In order to succeed, are you willing to work a demanding 60 to 70 hours a week, or will you choose work that affords leisure time to be with your family and friends and to pursue enjoyment outside of work?
- Do you want a career that contributes to society and the welfare of others?

These are all huge decisions and they need to be faced, the consequences considered and plans made as early as possible. Then, there is the whole issue of money.

- How much is enough?

- If you succeed in making a lot of money, what will you do with it?

- Are you willing to lie, cheat, and run over others in order to get ahead?

Here is a test for you to consider. Which would make you feel better about yourself?

- Driving a new Mercedes that everyone admires and envies or driving a Honda and using the savings to help feed a hungry family?

- To put it another way, would you rather be rich and famous or comfortable and generous?

Here are some suggestions I have found to be helpful:

- Become an expert.

- Find something you can do well and become a specialist at it. It makes no difference what it is—brain surgeon, rocket scientist, anthropology professor, plumber, carpenter, picture restorer, science teacher or bricklayer. If you are good at what you do, doing it will bring great satisfaction, joy and good feelings about yourself.

If you are unable to find a job that provides an opportunity to specialize in something you enjoy, then you have at least three options:

1. Take up a hobby that allows you to enjoy the fine arts, or other creative pursuits. Either learn to appreciate them or participate in them. Write, compose, play, sing, dance, plant a garden, become an expert on violets, create! You don't even have to be good at it, just enjoy the process and relish doing something creative.

2. Find a way to become proficient in the job you have and excel at it, even if you are not particularly fond of the work you have to do. Thomas Edison told us there is always a better way. Our job is to find it.

3. The luminous Barbara Brown Taylor, who writes as if her quill were the tip of an angel's wing, told me that what one decides to do is not as important as how it is done.

It seems to me that the really fortunate are those who both love their work and make a contribution to the world. These are the successes, not the Wall Street tycoons or captains of industry for whom building wealth may be the only goal. Consider fully, decide early, and find a productive and meaningful career.

The ideal career is one that combines something you love to do with earning a living. There are many examples, most of which involve something creative—acting, music, art, writing, and teaching. Unfortunately, occupations in some of these fields are few and far between.

As a result, many of us are forced into careers we dislike or find tedious, boring or well below our capabilities. Is there an inventive solution? I think so, and it goes like this: *if you can't find a way to turn your joy into a job, then find a way to turn your job into a joy!* Easier said than done? Perhaps, but here are some proven examples:

Simply try to come up with ways to make your work more enjoyable or more productive. I know of an office where they set weekly quotas. If the quotas are reached, employees may leave early on Friday afternoons.

Try to invent or create a better way to do your job or a better system for your company. Each of us has been blessed with the power of imagination, so use yours. Perhaps there's an invention imprisoned in your ancestral or unconscious brain. Another way to make a dull job more interesting is to team up with a co-worker to find better ways to get your jobs done. Combining ideas and efforts should bring you closer together. You may find that your two heads together can produce the output of three. Then ask for raises or promotions!

One final thought about turning your job into a joy. If you hate your boss, or even if you don't, try finding ways to make his or her job easier or better or both. Perhaps he or she will be promoted, move on, and you can fill the vacant position if you want it.

On a simpler level, no one particularly enjoys washing dishes, but believe it or not, there are ways to make it fun, even exciting. Turn it into a contest or a game, time yourself and then try to beat your own record, dream up better ways, create labor-saving devices. Who knows, you might set up a whole new industry! Even if you can't pull this off, you can take pride in doing the job well. It works for me; give it a try. The possibilities are limited only by your imagination! Uncork your genie.

While I am discussing the subject of gainful employment, this book's Web site contains some suggestions for adults as well as teens about getting a good job in the first place:

Religion and Philosophy

I have heard it said that philosophy is the attempt to reconcile religion and science, but many of the teenagers I have worked with seem to have little or no interest in religion, philosophy or science. They go to church only because their parents insist. They stop as soon as they are of age. Sunday school attendance is down. Why is this?

The young people I taught in Sunday school were mostly upper middle class and white. They did not pay much attention to the political emergence of the fundamentalist far Christian Right. They were too busy focusing on themselves, being popular, being "hot," and getting into a good college. They were bright and skeptical, often rejecting, if they ever held them, beliefs in the Bible stories they were taught as children: creation of the earth in seven days; original sin; virgin birth; healing the sick and lame; Jesus dying for our sins; and the resurrection of the body. They harbor doubts about miracles or the ability of prayer to change anything. How then are they to be reached?

Here are a few of the things that I found helpful. These young people, for the most part, had good minds, so I challenged them to think. Since it was, after all, a Sunday school class, I suggested we start with the Bible. I pointed out that there were at least four different ways to read the Bible: literally, figuratively, symbolically and historically. No one of these is necessarily better than another. They are simply different, and each way should be considered with care.

Taking the Bible Literally

We usually started with taking the Bible literally. Many people believe that every word in the Bible comes directly from God and is, therefore, to be accepted without question. This stance leaves little room for independent thought, especially regarding miracles; but I believe that individually and collectively we have a right to our own beliefs, and these should be respected.

I told students that one of the most interesting challenges to literalism lies in the interpretations of "turn the other cheek," "love your enemies," and "give all you have to the poor." The Quakers and Amish practice these commands literally, as do many Buddhist and Jainist sects; how about the rest of us?

Taking the Bible Figuratively

We next turn to figurative interpretations of Biblical stories and sayings. I urged my students not to, as the old German proverb goes, "throw out the baby with the bathwater." That is, if they could not accept literal interpretations, not to turn away from the rich and powerful meanings found in the beauties of biblical metaphor. For example, seven days in God's universe can be eons in ours; "virgin" can mean youthful purity; original sin can mean that we are all weak human beings and need spiritual help to find our way; Jesus dying on a cross can be looked at as his literal demonstration of one of his most profound sayings, "Greater love hath no man than this, that he lay down his life for his friends."

Lately, I have been pondering another interpretation of the reason for Jesus' crucifixion. The prevailing doctrine of Jesus as a paschal lamb being sacrificed as a "propitiation for the sins of the world" (1 John 2:2) seems antiquated and almost pagan to many of today's teens (and to many adults as well). How could a loving God ask that of his only son?

For me, Jesus' commandment to "love your enemies, bless them that curse you, do good to those that hate you, and pray for those who spitefully use you" is the most powerful saying of all time. It is also the most difficult. So when I think of Jesus hanging on the cross in excruciating agony and saying "Father, forgive them for they know not what they do," I am often moved to tears. And that for me is the real significance of the crucifixion.

As an aside, since I am a psychologist, I wonder about the commandment to "love our neighbors as ourselves." What if we don't love ourselves? It is relatively easy to love neighbors because they are usually like us, but what about loving our enemies and those who "spitefully use" us? Now, that's tough—so tough that the only way to achieve it may be through the strength of the Holy Spirit! Seldom, can we do it on our own.

Healing the sick and lame illustrates the power of faith and the spirit to conquer the infirmities of the flesh; the resurrection of the body may be seen as a figurative way of expressing the hope and faith that there is something beyond this earthly existence. Powerful stuff!

TAKING THE BIBLE SYMBOLICALLY

Looking at Biblical material symbolically provides still another means of gaining insight and strength from these ageless tales. Symbolism may be defined as a tangible or visible sign or representation of truths or ideals that are intangible or invisible. The Christian sacrament of communion or the Eucharist, for example, is defined as an "outward and visible sign of an inward and spiritual grace."

The Bible abounds with examples of symbolic expression: Abraham willing to sacrifice Isaac; Moses parting the waters; Joshua making the sun stand still; Jonah in the whale; the trials of Job; Jesus' miracles and healing; Paul's blindness—all vivid expressions of God's power and man's faith. Jesus' crucifixion and suffering, looked at symbolically, teach us that suffering and dying are necessary in order to be born again. We die to our old selves in order to be resurrected to our new selves.

TAKING THE BIBLE HISTORICALLY

Finally, reading the Bible as history provides a deeper understanding of our Judeo-Christian heritage. We can become grounded in the origins of tradition, custom and liturgies that remain with us today.

I told students that any or all of the ways of reading and interpreting the Bible can reveal profound truths that will enrich their own beliefs and knowledge. What is important is to study and learn and ask questions for themselves and not rely solely on the opinions and beliefs of others.

Next, I suggested they also learn all they can about other religions so that whatever beliefs they choose or reject for themselves will be based on as much knowledge as they can acquire. I recommended reading Genesis and other books of the Torah to learn where both Judaism and Christianity started and how their views are different and similar. I urged them to explore Hinduism and compare reincarnation with resurrection and being born again. Also, I asked them to investigate Buddhism to find the power of living in the here and now, focusing on and savoring one thing at a time, and finding peace inside themselves.

As an illustration, I told them about something I do at breakfast as often as I can. I usually eat a bowl of cereal with a sliced banana on it. I drink a cup of hot herbal tea and read the morning paper. I used to do these all at once and as a result, never fully appreciated any of them. Now, I eat the cereal first and relish every bite, chew the raisins and banana slices slowly, become aware of the different flavors of the bran, the raisins, the milk and the sugar substitute. This done, I peruse the paper as thoroughly as time permits, finishing up with an attempt at the scrambled word game. Finally, the pièce de résistance, I pour my cup of hot herbal tea and drink it slowly and lovingly until the very last drop. With this gentle start, I am relaxed, fulfilled and ready for the day. I realize that not all of us can do this every day, but every now and then it can be wonderful.

Now, let's get back to the subject. I advised my students to read translations of all or parts of the Koran or Qur'an. If they did not have time (their schedules were unbelievably full), I read them excerpts so they can compare versions of Paradise and Hell, punishment and forgiveness, love and hate, treatment of "infidels" and treatment of parents and women, and attitudes toward Christians and Jesus. All of us need to know these things as our worlds grow closer.

In the Christian religion I suggested they re-read the Sermon on the Mount and the Gospel of John. If they were skeptical of miracles, I asked them to consider what Jesus said and did. These are, at least in my opinion, more important than reading or listening to what others said or wrote about Him.

If they could not or would not accept the concept that Jesus was "the only son of God," I suggested they consider Him as the perfect example or embodiment of love. We are all sons and daughters of God, but Jesus set for us the ultimate example. Leo Tolstoy concluded that Jesus was human but that his words were divine.

I asked them to think about ideas like "God is love" or perhaps "love is God," "love those who hate you" and "sell all you have and give it to the poor" and to consider them literally, figuratively, or symbolically. We considered the questions, "What if there is no beyond, no after-life? If this life is all there is, would that change our behavior?" These thoughts led to some provocative and stimulating discussions.

On the subject of prayer, we discussed not whether God can change God's own laws of nature but whether God ever does. My own conclusions are that God alters circumstances by touching a person's divine spirit within, and so I pray that we can and will be used to do God's will. Instead of praying for peace, or the poor, or the sick, I think it is more effective that we pray that our own spirits be touched so that we will be instruments of that peace, or of feeding or healing. When we pray for others, I believe it to be important that they know it, so they can experience the power of our combined spirits. I have found that works when I know that someone is praying for me.

Lastly, we talked about the religion of the Native Americans and their marvelous belief in a "Great Spirit" and of the inter-relatedness of breath, smoke, and spirit. We discussed, also, the spirit within and the spirit without. I speculated with them about our sharing this universal and common spirit with all of humanity.

Summary

Throughout this chapter, I have discussed at length the place and power of spiritual presence in finding the self, in discovering spiritual sexuality, in fighting the addictive temptations of alcohol and drugs, in facing and over-coming debilitating emotional disturbances, in discovering one's place and contribution to this troubled world and, finally, in embracing a faith, belief or philosophy to guide each of us through the complexities, sufferings, and joys of our existence. These are my views and I hope that students and parents will at least consider them, knowing full well that their true guide is the spirit that lies both within and outside of them.

10
THE PIMPLE PARABLE

Once upon a time there was a beautiful princess. She had long, auburn hair, deep emerald green eyes, a figure a model would kill for, and her soft, clear skin was absolutely flawless. The perfect package, and she knew it.

Anyone that gorgeous had to be vain and, indeed, she was. Every morning she gazed contentedly into her mirror, delighted at the image she beheld. Life was good; she was admired and praised by all, including herself. Then one dreadful day she turned from the mirror in shock. A tiny pimple marred her otherwise perfect cheek. A blemish! A rude, ugly intruder ravaged her pristine pulchritude.

She was devastated. Nothing else mattered. Forget the crowning halo of her russet hair. Never mind the svelte figure or the cerulean eyes, or her otherwise glowing complexion. She saw only the angry, inflamed, repulsive imperfection, and focused on the tiny defect to the exclusion of all else. She remained upset, foul-tempered, and disagreeable until the pimple finally healed and disappeared. Then she worried obsessively that it might return.

Does this story sound like an exaggerated fairy tale, a fabrication? It is not. Unfortunately, this sort of event visits each of us nearly every day. I call it "The Pimple Parable". In my experience, the principles illustrated in this parable are facts of life along with hay fever, upset stomachs, and people who interrupt while others are speaking.

> **OFTEN WE CONCENTRATE ON A FLAW IN OTHER PEOPLE TO THE EXTENT THAT WE OVERLOOK THEIR POSITIVE QUALITIES.**

It has many facets, and here are a few examples:

My wife and I are dressing to go out. She praises my new suit, tells me I'm looking younger than ever, compliments me on my choice of tie, and then adds casually, "But aren't you getting a little soft around the middle?" That does it; forget the suit, my still-youthful look, and the tie. All I think about is that my pants suddenly feel tighter than they did before. My evening is off to a bad start.

If you pay attention, I think you'll discover that similar situations occur frequently in your life:

- Your boss gives you a review on your work—four "excellents" and one "needs improvement." What do you focus on?

- Your child brings home a report card filled with A and B grades and one C. What do you say to her?

- You write a little poem or a story and then ask a friend to critique it (The legendary Ernest Hemingway said all new writers want is praise, never criticism.). Your friend likes your work for the most part—"Yes, but there is this one line..." Do you remain friends?

- There's a scratch on your new car, a spot on your cheese, one bad dish in an otherwise splendid meal.

- Your therapist assesses your personality as excellent—except for this one small flaw.

- Your physician pronounces you fit, but "we better keep an eye on ..."

- You hear about a public servant with a near-perfect record except for ...

The list is endless. Oh yes, did you notice that these examples always begin with a "but?"

How do we deal with this unpleasant and persistent trait? Well, for openers, it is important to recognize the signs when they occur, as they always do. Recognition (oops, there I go again) helps us observe the experience with a sense of humor and not take it or ourselves too seriously.

Then, I have found it helpful to remember that praise makes us grow fat, content and pleased with ourselves. Negative criticism, when delivered in a constructive way, although often painful, helps us improve. At least, it does after we stop pouting and realize that our critic is probably right, rather brave, and actually doing us a favor.

Many therapists advocate a highly effective technique that they call "reframing." Reframing has been around a long time and has many names and forms: "positive thinking"; "cognitive re-structuring"; "making the best of it"; "looking on the sunny side"; and many others. These notions used to sound contrived to me, but no more. They work.

Reframing can find a purpose for the pimple and thereby reposition its victim's reaction:

- "The pimple (a real one) is nature's way of drawing poison from the skin, so it is healthy and only lasts a short time."
- "It could have been smallpox and left a lasting scar."
- "It's our body's way of keeping us beautiful people humble."

The Pimple Parable is not only inward-looking. Often we concentrate on a flaw in other people to the extent that we overlook their positive qualities. An example of that is the hapless child with the single "C" on her grade report or a public servant with a near-perfect record except for .... The phenomenon is not new. In King Henry VIII, Shakespeare noted "Men's evil manners live in brass; their virtues we write in water." And in Julius Caesar: "The evil that men do lives after them; the good is oft interred with their bones."

How can we avoid The Pimple Parable's dangerous traps? To a great extent it depends on how we feel about ourselves.

The higher our self-regard, the less likely we are to be trapped in The Pimple Parable's jaws. So, if The Pimple Parable applies to you, learn to recognize it, find the humor in it and benefit from it. Learn to prevent it from spoiling your enjoyment of all your wonderful attributes, including your own pristine pulchritude.

11
PLEASE! WE'RE "STRETCHES" NOT "SHRINKS!"

Our daughter, Lyn, has been an elementary school counselor for the past two decades. When she took the exam to become an LPC (Licensed Professional Counselor), we discussed counseling and psychotherapy at some length. Afterward I decided to put some thoughts in writing. Here are the results.

In 1969, for my graduate school's comprehensive exam, I prepared a paper exploring the field of psychotherapy. I must have read thirty to forty books on the subject. My favorite work (now long out of print) was by Helmut Kaiser, a contemporary of Sigmund Freud. The book, titled Effective Psychotherapy was marvelous. I have never forgotten its essence:

The key to effective psychotherapy is to be able to 'be with' the patient.

That's simple to say, but not so simple to do. Now, after more than forty years of practicing, I feel

> I CALL WHAT I DO "INTERPERSONAL EXPERIENTIAL" THERAPY. BY THIS I MEAN THAT I DO AS MUCH AS I CAN TO KEEP OUR CONVERSATIONS IN THE "HERE AND NOW."

every so often that I have been able to accomplish this, but not always and not with every patient.

What I have come to understand is that therapists should become so focused on the patient that they are able to "get inside" a patient's mind and body to the extent that the same thoughts and feelings are experienced simultaneously. When and if this happens, it can be a peak moment for both participants, and healing can begin.

To make these concepts clearer, I have found it useful to consider *sympathy* as "feeling for" the person, empathy as "feeling with" the person, and Kaiser's "*being with*" as "feeling like" the other person.

It may be helpful here to try to draw a distinction between psychotherapy and counseling. As I understand it, counseling often deals with the following:

- expert advice-giving
- conflict resolution
- recommendations for such things as education and career choices
- decision-making
- anger management
- anger elimination
- problem-solving for families and couples

Psychotherapy, on the other hand, focuses primarily on the following:

- emotions
- pathologies
- personality disorders
- life changes

Counseling and psychotherapy overlap in many areas. As a psychotherapist, my specialty has been primarily individual, couples, and family therapy. My early training involved a great deal of problem-solving and conflict-resolution techniques such as the Gestalt "empty chair," lists of "I appreciate and I resent," and "alter ego" exercises. Later, I became caught up in video feedback with couples and families, so they could see themselves in action, which eliminated a lot of denial and was quite effective. I experimented doing family and couples co-therapy with a female colleague; but, except with students or trainees, it is usually too expensive, although highly powerful. In the 1980s, I visited Jay Haley, in Washington, D.C., to observe his telephone supervisor techniques, but I preferred having the student doing the therapy in the same room with me.

As I have grown older and more experienced, I have come to believe ever more strongly in the place of emotions in psychotherapy. So instead of giving advice or helping to resolve conflicts, I have found that if emotions (especially anger—see Chapter 2) can be brought under control the individuals, couples, or families can solve very well most of their own problems. In doing so, they feel much more pleased with themselves and will probably come up with better solutions for those problems than I could ever give them. So, unless abuse or danger is involved, I will never tell a couple they should not be together. We may weigh alternatives and explore consequences, but that decision is theirs alone to make. Period!

Nineteenth century writer Oscar Wilde once said, "It is always a silly thing to give advice, but to give good advice is fatal." Here's why I believe he was right.

When you give advice several bad things can happen:

1. The advice is good but the person doesn't take it because it came from you, or she takes it and then makes sure it doesn't work (passive-aggressive). Other examples of passive-aggressive behavior are tardiness, not listening, agreeing to do something together and managing to spoil it for both participants, and failing to do something one of them has promised.

2. The advice is good; the person accepts it but feels bad because he didn't think of it himself.

3. The advice is bad, and the person blames the therapist.

4. The advice is bad, but the person blames herself for its failure and feels even worse.

Is giving advice ever appropriate? Sure, under these conditions:

- If people ask for advice after having been unsuccessful trying to find answers on their own.

- If the advice givers are experienced, trained and successful experts in their fields.

- If the advice is given in the form of training or instruction and not rendered in a mandatory way (e.g. "you should" or "you must"). It is highly important that the counselor/therapist always keep clearly in mind this distinction between instruction and advice.

- If the advice is given in the form of suggestions, alternatives, or choices, so that the receiver has a part in the decision-making. Whenever I forget my own advice and tell someone what to do, something undesirable usually happens.

- If neither direct advice nor letting people figure out their own solutions works, there are some subtle techniques ("sneaky smart") that can be successful. One of these is exploring alternatives together: "Have you ever thought of, or tried, this?"

Once I heard the master of humorous cognitive therapy, Donald Meichen-baum talk about indirect techniques such as telling the patient as follows: "Well, one time when I had a similar problem, I tried..." or "I once had a patient (or friend) who found that this worked." Meichenbaum said he would even resort to making up appropriate stories. I don't like this option, but the techniques do work because the person then can choose whether to try them, thus taking responsibility for the outcome.

MEDICATIONS

In graduate school, I was taught to steer away from psychotropic medications except in cases of psychosis. When I interned at a state hospital in Georgia, the primary medications used were phenothiazines, which were given to just about everyone. These powerful tranquilizers kept the patients subdued, which made the staff happy, but I don't remember seeing anyone improve. It was heart-breaking.

That was decades ago. Medications have changed drastically since then and so have my views. Now anti-psychotic drugs calm the troubled mind and allow the patient to assume a reasonably self-sustaining life. There are equally effective medicines available today for treating depression, anxiety, and anger. There is also a large body of research to show the extra effectiveness of these drugs when combined with psychotherapy. I know this to be true both as a therapist and as a patient.

I have told Lyn my personal views about the kind of therapist I try to be, or, at least, what works for me. And that brings us to another distinction between counseling and psychotherapy—time.

The counselor seldom enjoys the luxury of long-term, professional relationships, especially in public settings. A counselor's messages must be given quickly and strongly. Unfortunately, there is little opportunity for more than cursory follow-ups.

The psychotherapist, on the other hand, usually has sufficient time to explore the patient's background, history, personality and feelings. Thus begins the formation of a relationship. If that relationship is not given time to develop, in my experience, not much lasting personality change occurs in the patient.

I don't do cognitive or behavioral therapies (although I understand they can be quite effective in certain cases) primarily because they do things "to" the patients and not "with" them, thereby—I believe—reinforcing dependence. Also, Cognitive Behavior Therapy (CBT) is based on the premise that "thought controls feelings." In my experience, more often the opposite is true: improve the mood and positive thinking will follow.

I call what I do "interpersonal experiential" therapy. By this I mean that I do as much as I can to keep our conversations in the "here and now." I try to explore the kind of feelings, on both sides, that our patient-therapist relationship evokes, and to see how this exchange of feelings compares with the patient's real-world experiences. If those experiences are or have been unsatisfactory, we explore different ways of relating with each other that may result in different emotional outcomes.

For example, let's return to that old nemesis, anger. If something I have said or done provokes anger, I first want to find out why. What has been heard? How does that compare to other relationships? Why did the client *embrace anger* and how does this affect how he or she feels about himself or herself? That is all important stuff, and we don't usually wander back to childhood experiences or long histories of other unsuccessful relationships. Everything takes place right there, right then. If we find new methods of knowing each other, I may suggest trying these in outside relationships, but that choice is always left to the patient.

Staying with anger for a moment, I used to tell my graduate students: "If you become angry with a patient, it is always your fault, and you cannot build a successful relationship with that patient as long as you choose to remain angry. You must remember that the reason patients are in therapy is for you to help them learn to solve their own problems, not add to them." My students often fought this, but I still believe it to be true. On occasion, I have lost control and expressed my anger toward a patient. While my outburst may let patients experience how they affect others, it is seldom good therapy and can lead to disastrous consequences. It may show my human side, but it is not professional, and I was not practicing what I preach.

> IT IS THE JOB OF THE THERAPIST OR COUNSELOR TO EXPAND, NOT COMPRESS, THE PATIENT'S MIND, NOT TO TEACH THEM WHAT TO THINK BUT HOW TO THINK BETTER.

I believe that the key to bringing about change is the ability on the part of the therapist to find something to like about each patient. A therapist may not always be able to regard patients positively, but if we can't find something worthwhile, likeable, or even lovable, we will never be able to restore a patient's self-esteem. Patients must first feel good about themselves; that's the best way for them to bring about effective, positive changes. Change the feelings, and the behaviors will improve.

Now this is probably the toughest part about being a therapist. How can we find something to like in a person who has done despicable things? I have worked with child molesters, rapists, committers of incest, people who have deliberately hurt someone, spousal abusers, liars, thieves (including people who have kept their insurance money and never paid me) and people who are just mean-spirited. How can we deal with them positively?

First, we must learn to separate the person from the behavior. Then it is up to us to investigate how the patient got that way and help him or her try to fix it. That's our job. If we can't teach ourselves to become accepting and non-judgmental, we don't belong in the psychotherapy business.

I don't think that either counseling or psychotherapy is necessarily better or more important than the other; they are simply different; and, when done well, both can be effective. So to summarize: in my experience, counseling is primarily concerned with behavior change, problem-solving, career selection, advising, instructing, and conflict resolution. It is relatively short-term and does not necessarily involve an emotional relationship between client and counselor.

Psychotherapy includes some of the above but is more focused on character or personality change and uses emotions as its primary tool. It is of longer duration and deals with patient-therapist relationships.

Oh yes, about this "stretch" versus "shrink" business. It is the job of the therapist or counselor to expand, not compress, the patient's mind, not to teach them what to think but how to think better. This means looking at their lives in new ways, stretching not shrinking their imagination—growth not diminution.

As I see it, one of my jobs as a therapist is to help the patient dispose of accumulated garbage and baggage, pull out the "shadow cork," and help liberate the genie that is always waiting there (see Chapter 4).

Finally, I thought you might enjoy knowing at least one definition of the difference between a psychiatrist and a psychologist. The answer used to be "about $10 an hour." This is no longer true; so my dear friend and colleague psychiatrist Albert Davis, M.D., helped me come up with this one. First, psychiatrists are trained in medicine; psychologists are trained in behavior and relationships. Second, psychiatrists are trained to talk; psychologists are trained to listen. Third, psychiatrists don't get to wear sandals.

12
AFTER WORDS ABOUT AFTERWARDS

Now, Dear Reader, you have read a good bit of what I have learned during more than forty years as a psychotherapist, and I would love to hang around to see what happens during the next forty years. Since that is not likely, here is what I wish:

1. Our best scientific minds would turn toward enhancing rather than destroying life and replace nuclear fission and fossil fuels with practical, nuclear fusion that has no toxic waste.

2. Universal voluntary birth control methods would be made available worldwide, at no cost, in order to achieve population stabilization.

3. Stem cell and genetic engineering research would provide healthy bodies and minds and eliminate diseases, birth defects and much pain and suffering.

4. Organic agriculture advances would serve to produce unlimited food supplies so that starvation would no longer exist.

5. Improved electronic techniques would turn gadgetry from amusement more toward education and the acquisition of skills and so provide jobs and services that would eliminate poverty and raise worldwide standards of living.

6. Finally, I hope that everyone will learn to replace anger with creativity so that differences may be settled with discussion, not argument, and that disputes may be resolved by "inventive alternatives" rather than combat.

**THANK YOU FOR YOUR PATIENT ATTENTION.
UNTIL WE MEET AGAIN, FAREWELL AND "SHARE JOY."**

Thomas Schneider

GLOSSARY

Ancestral Unconscious: A companion concept to Jung's collective unconscious. Here are stored memories, talents, revelations, inspirations, and other attributes unique to each individual. This repository is located, presumably, in our lower hippocampus.

Anger: The Webster Dictionary defines anger as "a strong feeling of displeasure and usually of antagonism." In this book I have divided the emotion of anger (which can be experienced on a scale ranging from irritation, annoyance, peevishness, and indignation to rage and fury) into three distinct categories: reactive, responsive and retentive.

Archetype: Jung (1964) referred to these as "archaic remnants" or "primordial images."

Collective Unconscious: Jung (1964) defined this as "the part of the psyche that transmits the common psychological inheritance of mankind."

Comfort: Having all that you need to be content and secure (see luxury).

Embracing Anger: The anger we hold onto and which holds onto us when we feel we have been hurt, wronged, diminished, or insulted.

Genie: A private spiritual force residing in our ancestral unconscious with three primary functions: first, to help disintegrate our "shadow cork," second, to become a vehicle to assist our under-conscious attributes in emerging into consciousness, and third, to act as a voice to help us hear and understand what these qualities have to say to us.

Idiotype: Inherited instincts, talents, or skills specific to the individual.

Intermittent Reinforcement: The learning theory that as long as chance or hope is present, organisms will persist in continuing certain behaviors.

Inventive Alternative Method: Not a compromise; compromise seldom satisfies anyone. It is a new solution to which both parties have contributed equally and with which both are satisfied.

Luxury: Possessing more than is needed to be comfortable. (See Comfort)

Moderation Generation: A suggested societal movement to extol the values of sobriety, not so much as a moral issue, but as a scientific one. Specifically, to provide information on the toxic effect of alcohol and drugs in inhibiting the growth of new brain cells and the nourishing effect of critical thinking in the growth of new cells.

OCCP: Obsessive Compulsive Creative Personality. A personality type in which an individual has transformed his or her obsessive/compulsive traits into useful, constructive, creativity or inventiveness.

Pimple Parable: A facet of the human condition in which we allow a small blemish to spoil the beauty that surrounds it.

Precision time out: Systematic application of fundamental learning theory principles such as: rewarding positive behavior is always more effective than punishing negative behavior; intermittent reinforcement always leaves a window of hope and is extremely difficult to extinguish; negative consequences permit involvement by the recipient; and relentless consistency is the key to successful parental influence.

Pro-qual: A suggested abbreviation for pro-quality of life. As an alternative attitude to pro-life or pro-choice, it considers the ramifications of bringing a new life into a world that doesn't want it, can't properly care for it, and can't support it. That attitude, if assumed, can lessen a prospective mother's guilt and soften society's views toward abortion.

Shadow Cork: A compressed mass of debilitating negative emotions held together by the glue of anger and blocking access to and egress from our ancestral unconscious.

Spiritual Sexuality: This is the type of intimacy that discovers the person behind the sexual façade and leads to a "caring above carnality" union of two souls.

Stretch and Shrink: Psychologists, psychiatrists, social workers and psychotherapists have long been tagged "head-shrinker" or "shrink." While cute, these sobriquets do an injustice to these trained professionals. Their job is to expand, not contract, the patient's mind and consciousness. Therefore, the term "stretch" would be not only kinder but far more appropriate.

Under-Conscious: A third level of consciousness in addition to the conscious and sub-conscious. This level, presumably located in the lower hippocampus, contains both Jung's "collective unconscious" and an individual's "ancestral unconscious."

REFERENCES

Better World Campaign. (2008). *U.S. Funding for the UN: An Overview.* Retrieved August 17, 2009 from http://www.betterworldcampaign. org/issues/funding/us-funding-for-the-un-an-overview.html

Culbertson, P. (2000). *Caring for God's People: Integrating Spirituality Into Pastoral Counseling.* Minneapolis: Augsburg Fortress.

Einstein, A. (1956). *Out of My Later Years.* New York: Citadel Press.

Emerson, R. W. (1909). *Essays.* New York: Collier.

Gottman, J. (1999). *The Seven Principles for Making Marriage Work.* New York: Three Rivers Press.

Greenberg, L. & Goldman, R. (2008). *Emotion-Focused Couples Therapy.* Washington: American Psychological Association.

Jung, C. (1964). *Man and His Symbols.* London: Aldus Books, Ltd.

Jung, C. (1995). *Memories, Dreams, Reflections.* New York: HarperCollins.

Kaiser, H. (1965). *Effective Psychotherapy: The Contribution of Hellmuth Kaiser.* Ed. Louis B. Fierman. New York: Free Press.

Maslow, A. (1954). *Motivation and Personality.* New York: Harper.

Meichenbaum, D. (1977). *Cognitive Behavior Modification: An Integrative Approach.* New York: Springer.

Olson, D. & Olson, A. (2000). *Empowering Couples.* Minneapolis: Life Innovations.

Taylor, B. B. (2009). *An Altar in the World.* New York: Harper Collins.

Taylor, C. (1999). *Premarital Guidance.* Minneapolis: Augsberg.

INDEX

conscience, 46
conscious, 5, 28, 29, 54, 55, 56, 91, 92
Consequences, Reinforcement and
    Punishment, 46
consistency, 47, 50, 51, 92
contagious, 12, 23, 34
contempt, 38, 40
contiguity, 47
contingencies, 46, 48
contraception, 57, 58, 60
contribution, x, 30, 31, 74, 78, 93
control, 8, 19, 23, 33, 35, 38, 40, 46, 47,
    65, 70, 84, 86, 87
cooperation, 14, 25, 47
cooperative, 20, 23
counseling, 37, 39, 83, 84, 86, 88, 93
counselor, 33, 39, 40, 53, 83, 85, 86, 88
couples, xi, 11, 13, 37, 38, 41, 42, 84, 93
creative, 14, 19, 64, 69, 73, 74, 92
criticism, 1, 9, 34, 38, 40, 41, 80
crucifixion, 76
Culbertson, Philip, 37, 93
curiosity, 24, 49, 72

D

danger, 57, 61, 62, 64, 72, 85
Davis, Albert, v, x, 88
decision-making, 38, 67, 84, 85
defensive, 36
depressed, 33, 39, 68
depression, 1, 5, 7, 8, 12, 24, 28, 43, 55,
    67, 68, 70, 86
Descartes, Rene, 28, 55
despair, 6
dignity, v, 38, 40
diminished, 5, 6, 12, 64, 67, 91
diminishment, 7, 12, 24
disagreements, 38, 46, 100
disappointment, 5, 14, 25
diseases, 58, 89
dissipate, 36, 41
dress code, 57, 60
drinking, 33, 38, 41, 65, 66, 67
drugs, 40, 57, 58, 61, 62, 63, 66, 72, 78,
    86, 91
    anti-psychotic, 86
dual personality, 6

E

economics, 49
education, vi, 54, 56, 57, 62, 71, 72, 84, 89
education, careers and money, 71
Egyptians, 18
Einstein, Albert, 28, 93
electronic, iii, 49, 63, 89
embarrassment, 5, 70
Emerson, Ralph Waldo, 8, 20, 93
emotions, v, vi, 1, 2, 3, 6, 7, 8, 12, 13, 19,
    23, 24, 28, 29, 38, 40, 42, 54, 58,
    59, 60, 67, 68, 70, 71, 78, 84, 87,
    88, 91, 92, 93, 100
emptiness, 14, 25
English, 19
enjoyment, 14, 25, 71, 72, 81
escalates, 12
eternal verities, 28, 55
Europeans, 18
evolutionary, 1, 12, 70
excuses, 7, 50, 51
exercises, 19, 20, 21, 48, 62, 64, 84
expectations, 40, 42, 50
experiential, 41, 83, 87
external stimulants, 61, 63

F

facilitator, 19
failure, 11, 68, 85
faith, 17, 38, 42, 76, 78
family government, 45
fatigue, 5, 7, 12, 24
fear, 5, 6, 7, 8, 12, 18, 20, 24, 28, 55, 68,
    70
feelings, v, 3, 5, 6, 8, 12, 14, 25, 28, 33,
    34, 35, 36, 40, 42, 51, 54, 55, 60,
    70, 73, 83, 86, 87
flames, 6, 14, 25
flaw, 79, 80, 81
food, 21, 50, 51, 61, 63, 89
forgiveness, 7, 39, 43, 77
fragility, 40
fraternities, 66
Freud, 1, 60, 83
frustration, 5, 6
fulfillment, 14, 25, 30, 31
fury, 6, 91

G

gambling, 51, 61, 62
genetic, 5, 68
genetic engineering, 89
genie, iv, v, xi, 13, 27, 29, 30, 42, 55, 56,
    74, 88, 91
uncorking, v, 13, 27, 30, 56, 74
Georgia, iii, iv, v, vi, 63, 71, 86, 100
Georgia Tech, 71
Gestalt, 84
GOcabulary®, 8, 64
God, 40, 43, 55, 63, 75, 76, 78, 93
Gottman, John M., 41, 43
grades, 48, 80
Greenberg, Leslie S., 41, 43, 93
grudge, 6, 12, 39
guilt, 6, 7, 12, 24, 43, 57, 58, 59, 60, 69,
    70, 92

H

Haley, Jay, 84
happiness, 9, 30, 56, 69, 70
Harkins, Rev. Bill, 37
Harkins, Vickie, 58
healing, 14, 18, 33, 35, 75, 76, 78, 83
heat, 3, 42
Hebrew, 19
hippocampus, 28, 29, 67, 91, 92
homemaking, 38, 43
hostility, 19, 43
household, 47, 49, 50
humiliating, 38, 46, 70
humor, 7, 9, 12, 24, 54, 66, 67, 80, 81, 86
humors, v
hurt, 1, 5, 7, 12, 15, 24, 34, 40, 42, 66,
    88, 91

I

identities, 20
ideotypes, 28, 29
ignorance, 8, 20
inflammatory, 11, 12, 35
inspiration, 30, 56, 91
insult, 5, 6, 7, 12, 15, 30, 67, 91
integrity, 69
intermittent explosive disorder, 6
intrusion, 5
intuitive, 41
inventive, 27, 64, 66, 74, 92

inventive alternative, 11, 13, 14, 17, 16,
    18, 19, 20, 21, 23, 24, 25, 89, 91,
    100
Iranians, 18
Isaac, 76
Islam, 7, 12, 24
isolation, 7, 12, 24
Israelis, 18

J

Jainist, 92
Jesus, 18, 19, 75, 76, 78
Job (Bible), 76
job, 38, 47, 68, 71, 72, 73, 74, 76, 77, 88,
    89, 92
Jonah, 76
Jordanians, 18
Joshua, 76
Judaism, 17, 77
Judeo-Christian, 77
judges, 59
judgmental, 34, 37, 38, 69, 88
Jung, C.G., iv, v, 28, 55, 91, 92, 93

K

Kaiser, Helmut, 83, 84
King Henry VIII, 81
knowledge, 8, 20, 28, 29, 48, 49, 72, 77
Koop, C. Everett, 81
Koran. See Qur'an

L

Lebanese, 18
legislators, 59
Leyburn, James, 71
liberate, 14, 30, 56, 88
liberating creativity, 13, 24
limbic, 28
listen, 30, 53, 56, 88
listener, 35, 36, 42, 49
listening, 33, 35, 55, 56, 78, 85
liturgies, 77
loss, 5, 68
love, vii, 5, 8, 9, 14, 18, 38, 41, 42, 43,
    53, 55, 58, 59, 60, 69, 72, 74, 75,
    76, 77, 78, 89
loyalty, 59
lust, 59

Don't keep this book a secret. Share, share, share!

Buy additional copies of *Breaking Anger's Embrace* for individuals, book clubs or other groups.

Information available at: www.breakingangersembrace.com.

BREAKING ANGER'S EMBRACE
and Other Insights on the Human Condition

Thomas Schneider, Ph.D., is a life member of the American Psychological Association, a clinical member and approved supervisor for the American Association of Marriage and Family Therapists, a member of the American Association of Psychotherapists, and a Fellow of the Georgia Psychological Association.

In *Breaking Anger's Embrace*, he helps readers explore why we become angry, and what we can do to first counter and then eliminate an emotion that can be very destructive.

During more than 40 years of counseling individuals, couples, families, and organizations, Dr. Schneider has discovered that anger is usually a strong undercurrent in troubled lives and relationships. Also, because he has observed that anger management techniques have limited success, he is offering new approaches for breaking anger's embrace altogether.

Dr. Schneider focuses on three concepts to break anger's embrace: probing the ancestral unconscious, discovering individual creativity and liberating that creativity to produce what he calls "inventive alternatives." He believes that by using his *Inventive Alternatives Method*©, individuals, couples, families and organizations can eliminate their own anger.

In an era when rage, conflicts and disagreements threaten personal relationships, communities and nations, *Breaking Anger's Embrace* is a book whose time has come.

www.ingramcontent.com/pod-product-compliance
Lightning Source LLC
LaVergne TN
LVHW091159080426
835509LV00006B/750